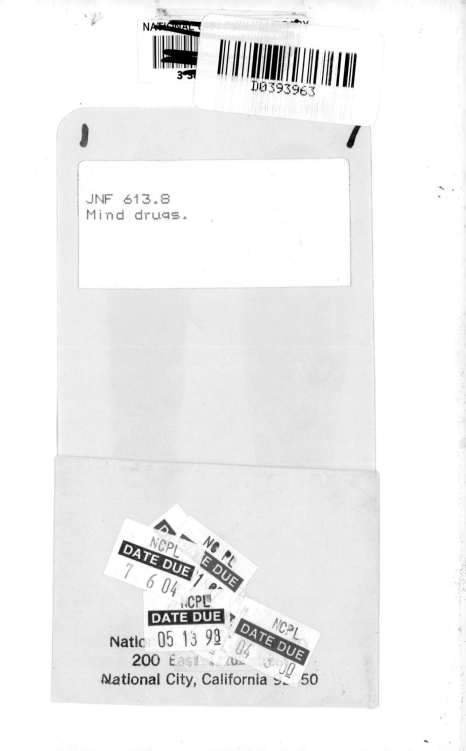

D0393963

MIND DRUGS

FIFTH EDITION

MIND
DRUGS

FIFTH EDITION

edited by
Margaret O. Hyde

DODD, MEAD & COMPANY
New York

Copyright © 1968, 1972, 1974, 1981, 1986 by Margaret O. Hyde
All rights reserved
No part of this book may be reproduced in any form
without permission in writing from the publisher
Distributed in Canada by
McClelland and Stewart Limited, Toronto
Manufactured in the United States of America
1 2 3 4 5 6 7 8 9 10

Library of Congress Cataloging-in-Publication Data

Mind drugs.

   Bibliography: p.
   Includes index.
   Summary: Leading authorities on drugs discuss the use, abuse,
and the effects of marijuana, alcohol, LSD, heroin, cocaine, PCP,
and other drugs and the alternatives to drug use.
   1. Substance abuse—United States—Juvenile literature.
2. Youth—United States—Substance use—Juvenile literature.
[1. Drugs. 2. Drug abuse] I. Hyde, Margaret O. (Margaret
Oldroyd), 1917-   . [DNLM: 1. Substance Abuse—popular works.
2. Substance Dependence—popular works.   WM 470 M663]
HV4999.2.M56 1986   613.8   86-11487
ISBN 0-396-08813-9

To Anita Townley

CONTENTS

NOW THE GOOD PART BEGINS:

MIND DRUGS

FIFTH EDITION

MIND DRUGS: TODAY AND TOMORROW

Margaret O. Hyde

Mrs. Hyde has written more than fifty books for young people, including *Know About Drugs*, a book for younger boys and girls. Other recent titles are *Sexual Abuse: Let's Talk About It; AIDS: What Does It Mean to You?; Missing Children;* and *Cancer in the Young.*

The drugstore for chemicals that affect the mind has grown into a giant supermarket with as many as 25,000 illicit drugs being sold at an estimated cost of billions of dollars a year. The drugs that are used and abused change from place to place and from time to time, but the quest for chemical calm and pleasure continues. New drugs have appeared on the scene, and some very old ones, such as cocaine, have increased in popularity.

The most commonly used mind drugs—caffeine, nicotine, and alcohol—were not always recognized as drugs. Coffee and tea drinkers are countless, about 50 million people in the United States smoke, and about 20 million people are either alcoholics or have alcohol problems.

Illegal drugs, used individually and in combination, continue to be explored both in the laboratory and on the "street." The variety of drugs, ages of users, and the methods and degree of use are all part of the changing drug scene. For example, Tom, age ten, carries vodka in the thermos of his lunch box. Jane, a thirteen-year-old, has tried marijuana at parties. Five seventh graders are arrested for selling cocaine. A committee of the student government tries to help authorities who are working to prevent the sale of marijuana and hashish on the school grounds.

Some parents, who were children in the sixties, find that their own children are embarrassed by their use of marijuana. These same parents express great concern about the abuse of drugs by ballplayers, rock stars, and actors. No one knows how many young people are influenced by the drug abuse of these adults, but it is known that a great many young people experiment with drugs that affect the mind and some of them find themselves in deep trouble.

Around the world for thousands of years, humans have altered their way of thinking and feeling by using drugs of numerous kinds. The pleasure seeker, the patient whose pain is diminished, the experimenter, the escapist who uses drugs as a crutch: all are people whose brains respond in a way that is still not fully understood. But today there is a great effort toward understanding and there is some progress. There is some light in the dark tunnel of confusion that surrounds the mind-drug mystique.

New approaches to drug problems consider drug-taking from the standpoint of use as well as abuse. They also consider the emotions, drives, and goals of human beings. The old scare tactics based on the ignorance that bred fear have been largely discarded in favor of research programs aimed at learning more of the truth about drugs. Some prevention programs abide by the theme of "profit from mistakes."

Who is an addict? What does addiction mean? If a person orients his life around a certain drug, if he feels that he cannot live without it, and if he suffers physical symptoms when the drug is withdrawn, he could be classified as a drug addict. Many people would automatically assume the drug to be heroin, although there are more people addicted to the drug alcohol and to other drugs.

Might not some cigarette smokers qualify as addicts? Might not some golfers, compulsive eaters, and a wide variety of people whose lives center about certain other things or who cannot live comfortably without these behaviors be considered addicts?

Actually, in the case of mind drugs, definitions are far less important than people. Researchers, medical doctors, and society in general are looking at the problem of drug abuse more from a "people"- or patient-oriented point of view.

The abuser who is considered a patient rather than a criminal is benefiting from the new look at mind drugs. First the "drunken bum" was accepted as a sick person and became known as an alcoholic. Today there is a tendency for this attitude to extend to abusers of other kinds of drugs. Large numbers of people are more concerned with the search for causes of drug abuse and for better ways of rehabilitation rather than simply considering punishment the only answer to the problem. Certainly, there is a great need for more understanding.

Understanding would be easier if there were less controversy and confusion in the drug scene, both in the laboratory and in the underground. The marijuana controversy, for example, includes arguments that range from statements that weekly marijuana use is extremely dangerous to statements that marijuana is 100 percent safe. Neither is considered true by health experts. However, some have changed from a relaxed attitude toward marijuana to expressions of deep concern because of the greater potency of the smoked material, the greater frequency of use, and the increasing youthfulness of users.

Many young Americans are showing an increasing interest in their own health and this has carried over to the use of marijuana. The dramatic shift in attitude in the last seven years is evident in the results of a recent Institute for Social Research Survey. It indicated that the proportion of senior high school students smoking marijuana daily has been halved, dropping to 5 percent. Occasional use dropped by a third, to 25 percent.

Most authorities agree that regular use of any intoxicant that blurs reality and encourages a kind of psychological escapism makes growing up more difficult. Who is an authority? While some users and abusers are well versed in the language of the scene, their scientific knowledge of what a certain amount of a drug will do to the nervous system of a human being is slim. To them, physiology and the uniqueness of individual reactions remain largely a mystery. Such self-styled authorities may be unaware that what happens to one person who takes a drug may be very different from what happens to another. In addition to this, the way a drug acts on any mind varies with the amount of the dose, the set, or time at which it is taken, the purity, and other factors. And in the drug underground, the true contents of the drug are often a question. Awareness of the above is increasing among the young people who are exposed to the world of illegal drugs. Many of today's young people are more sophisticated than their older brothers and sisters. Most of them are intelligent, idealistic, and full of promise for the unsolved problems of today and tomorrow. They can play a large part in solving drug abuse problems by recognizing experts and learning from them. The people who have contributed to this book have a wide variety of experiences with the problems about which they write and are well qualified to express their opinions. Several write about the same drug and about drug abuse from different viewpoints.

No one expects the illegal use of drugs that stimulate or depress brain activity to disappear. Some experts hope for a smoke-free society by the turn of the century, but they believe that alcohol will probably continue to be the major drug of abuse. The "designer drugs," synthetic drugs that are potent versions of drugs derived from plant sources, are often lethal. Combinations of drugs, such as the use of alcohol or heroin to calm the excitement from cocaine use, are increasing on the scene. As efforts to suppress drug trafficking grow, education for the prevention of drug abuse and treatment for the victims continues to need increased support.

People will continue to experiment with drugs that

produce different sensations, to reach for drugs that provide temporary solace from anxiety and depression, and to seek instant rewards without knowledge of long-term consequences. However, many surveys indicate that there is a growing aversion among young people to cigarettes, alcohol, and most illicit drugs. This loss in popularity in the face of widespread availability indicates that some drug abuse can be dealt with effectively through education.

The amount of drug abuse tends to rise and fall from year to year, and no one can accurately predict what the future will bring. While surveys showed a decrease in the abuse of most drugs for a period of five years, a University of Michigan survey of new high school graduates that was issued in the fall of 1985 found overall use of drugs slightly higher. As in other recent years and in numerous other studies, cocaine use appeared significantly higher. In a New York State survey, wide drug use was found among children before they entered seventh grade, a time when children are in the midst of a crucial psychological, physical, and emotional developmental period.

Surely, the clouds that surround the area of drug abuse have hardly begun to clear. There are no easy answers. Perhaps there are still more questions than answers, but the situation is being attacked on many fronts, such as the medical, social, economic, and legal. Drug abuse is being recognized as part of the big problem of real values.

Each drug abuser has taken his or her journey to "nowhere" for personal, complex reasons. Bringing the abuser home requires many bridges, and a great deal of understanding on the part of each individual who helps. It requires a tremendous amount of money and education of young and old so that all people realize that the problem of drug abuse is their problem, the problem of everyone who lives in today's world.

CONTEMPORARY PATTERNS OF YOUTH AND DRUG ABUSE

David E. Smith, M.D.

Dr. David E. Smith is founder and medical director of the Haight-Ashbury Free Medical Clinics, Associate Clinical Professor of Toxicology, University of California, San Francisco, and is the research director at the Merritt Peralta Institute Chemical Dependency Recovery Hospital in Oakland, California. As a Clinical Toxicologist and expert in chemical dependency, he has been involved in the new medical specialty of addictionology, the study and treatment of addiction. He is president of the *Journal of Psychoactive Drugs*.

Drug abuse may be defined as the use of a psychoactive drug to the point where it seriously interferes with an individual's health or economic or social functioning. Any drug abuse pattern is a complex interaction of physical, psychological, pharmacological, and social and cultural variables. Youthful drug abuse is one of the most controversial aspects of contemporary American society, despite the fact that psychoactive drug use per se is found throughout all the social and economic levels of our culture. For example, the President's National Commission on Marijuana and Drug Abuse determined that the number-one drug problem in the United States was the abuse of alcohol, a widely used legal drug that most people in America don't even consider to be a drug. The number-two drug abuse problem in the United States also revolves around a legal drug, namely tobacco, which if smoked on a regular basis substantially contributes to health problems such as lung cancer and heart disease. Unfortunately, when people discuss drug abuse in general or in a youth population they exclude the widespread abuse of legal drugs such as alcohol and tobacco. This chapter will focus on the abuse of psychoactive drugs defined by society as illegal and on contemporary patterns of drug use and abuse.

Prior to the 1960s and the 1970s patterns were relatively constant and predictable. "Illegal" drugs were confined to certain racial, ethnic, and philosophical minorities. Most often these were submerged within the urban ghettos. Most of the white middle class confined themselves to traditional mood-altering, or psychotropic, drugs such as cigarettes, alcohol, and certain prescription drugs during the "Silent '50s." Contemporary drug abuse patterns have shifted so dramatically and have become so widespread that at the present time the only thing that we can predict for sure about the drug scene is that it will change.

Society's view of drug abuse is beginning to change. No longer is it acceptable to label mildly psychoactive chemicals such as alcohol and nicotine as "nondrugs" and then insist that drug abuse occurs only in youth culture. Through a mixture of miseducation and ever-present puritanical reliance upon law, order, and punishment to regulate morality, the individual drug user is viewed by many people as a criminal and not as a patient. This attitude further alienates those young people who enter into the drug culture.

The Haight-Ashbury Free Medical Clinic and similar organizations have developed across the country in response to what was an increasing need of a growing alienated youth population. These community-based drug treatment programs have outpatient medical and psychiatric facilities that deal with new patterns of drug use, recognizing that "love needs care." People who are abusing drugs need sympathetic, nonpunitive, and professionally competent places where they can feel comfortable and still receive the care they need.

During nineteen years of operation the Haight-Ashbury Free Medical Clinic has seen over a million young people seeking help for a variety of health problems, many of which are associated with the abuse of illegal drugs. In addition, I have had the opportunity to talk with young people in many communities across the United States and it is this combined clinical experience that will serve as a basis for this chapter on youth and drug abuse.

PHASES OF YOUTHFUL DRUG USE

Many of today's young people find themselves exposed to an overwhelming number of newly available psychoactive drugs. They pass through various stages of use and some continue on to abuse. Since each person is different, one cannot make overall reasons for entering the drug scene, but for those who do, the majority of adolescent drug patterns can be basically defined in three phases. They are: (1) early experimental use, (2) periodic recreational use, and (3) some progression to compulsive drug abuse.

A clinic like the Haight-Ashbury Free Clinic is geared to deal with such problems as acute drug reactions. These occur most frequently in the experimental phase. Many young people sample illegal drugs, not realizing that a majority of "street" samples are "not as advertised." For example, illicit "mescaline," upon chemical analysis, may actually be LSD, a form of amphetamine known as DOM (STP), or PCP (Sernyl, a potent animal anesthetic). "THC" may also be PCP.

"Bad" drugs and peer group pressure toward indiscriminate experimentation have contributed greatly to the increase in adverse reactions. The vast majority experiment with drugs out of curiosity and peer group pressure. The increased availability of all drugs and peer pressure to try something new play an important part in the changing pattern of drug abuse. Most young people initially use a certain drug not because they are mentally ill or because it was forced on them by an illegal dealer but because drugs are a common topic of conversation. Young people are naturally curious, and very importantly they want to "belong" to a particular group. To demonstrate the severity of this widespread drug experimentation, a survey done at the Haight-Ashbury Free Clinic indicated that 40 percent of our patient population had taken a pill one or more times and didn't know what the drug was. Peer group pressure was a major factor in this uninformed, casual drug experimentation.

The Haight-Ashbury Free Medical Clinic, the first of over 500 free clinics, many of which are still active either as free or community clinics or in other forms of community medical service, was established in June of 1967 as a crisis-oriented response to the wave of transient and migratory alienated youth that flocked to the Haight-Ashbury district of San Francisco during the middle '60s. Initially the clinic was to treat the medical problems of alienated youth and to give emergency treatment to people with adverse LSD reactions. Psychedelics were the drugs of choice at that time, and young people who were seeking to find themselves through the use of such powerful drugs had a great mistrust for established health agencies. Since this group, popularly known as hippies, was seeking an alternative way of life, it was only natural that when they developed physiological and psychological problems they would seek alternative modes of treatment, and so they came in large numbers to the clinic.

We soon found, however, that many of these young people used psychoactive drugs in a destructive fashion. In addition to dealing with medical problems related to drug abuse (e.g., hepatitis, abscesses, and cellulitis), we began to offer psychological counseling and aftercare services, which were necessary for patients who had had bad LSD trips or who were plagued by the depression and impairment of function that inevitably seem to follow the excessive use of psychedelics.

Numbers and figures alone do not answer the question, "Who are the people served by an organization such as the Haight-Ashbury Free Medical Clinc?" Saying it is obvious that we serve "junkies" or "freaked-out acid heads," or discussing statistics doesn't really answer this basic question. *Clients are individual human beings with their own histories and sets of human characteristics.* Once the junkie life style and the drug are removed, the individual is revealed as unique, and any treatment program must be tailored to the patient's specific needs with great care. Only to the extent that similarities can be found in human nature can we lump our clients together and speak of them as a class. *No drug is in and of itself good or bad.* Drug abuse is defined by the destructive manner in which people use a drug, and the clinic relates to people problems, not just to drug problems. The following two cases demonstrate the success and failure of a "people-oriented" drug program like that of the clinic.

Case 1. Stan, a twenty-seven-year-old white male, came to the Haight-Ashbury neighborhood in the summer of 1967. He had grown up in a primarily middle-class setting and earned a liberal arts degree at the University of California. For about two years Stan lived in the Haight, taking LSD on a weekly basis and supporting himself by selling LSD and marijuana. The carnival atmosphere of the Haight in '67 was part of his experience and the first year was primarily one of newfound enjoyment and discovery. After a year or so things began to change both from within and from without. Just as curiously as the Haight had bloomed into the

Summer of Love, it was for many beginning to wilt into waste, paranoia, violence, and despair. Stan found himself beginning to show some of the typical symptoms of repeated acid use as well as the effects of the changing times. He became more withdrawn emotionally and socially. His own alienation and poor sense of identity became almost unbearable.

One of the routines that Stan had established for himself was taking his dog for a walk in the park. On his way he would pass the Psychological Services section of the Free Clinic on Clayton Street. He had debated with himself several times whether or not he should go in and ask for help. Finally one day, while feeling particularly depressed and lost, he decided to go inside.

Most probably if the clinic had not been located in the neighborhood he would have waited until his situation became intolerable before seeking help. Easy entry, both geographical and emotional, is a major factor in early case-finding. Another element, probably even more important, is that Stan was aware of the clinic's reputation for being sympathetic and responsive to the problems of long-haired hippies.

Upon entering the clinic he felt even more reassured by the generally hip atmosphere of the people and the place. Stan was assigned a counselor and for close to a year he came in once or twice a week to talk with him. Part of his therapy developed into the formation of daily routines and the limitation of sensory stimuli. This is often necessary to combat the inability to perceive spatial relationships and the untogetherness produced by excessive use of LSD. Also, attention was paid to focussing on his own body and physical health. Stan quit smoking cigarettes during this time and became active in sports again. Another important part of the therapy dealt with "direction," both vocational and emotional. With active support from his counselor Stan applied for and got a job working with emotionally disturbed children and later came back to the clinic as a counselor in the Rehabilitation Project.

Case 2. John and George are two white males, aged twenty-five and thirty respectively, who grew up in a large Midwestern city. Both are from lower middle-class families and were acquainted for about ten years in that same city. Both had always done well in their studies and were very popular in and away from school. Although neither of their families had much money they felt they were never really deprived of anything economically or socially. George started smoking marijuana at the age of twenty-two and John began at eighteen. For the next four years George stuck with marijuana and alcohol while John began to experiment with other drugs, including marijuana, LSD and other psychedelics, methamphetamine ("speed"), and finally heroin.

John left home during this time and ventured to the West Coast while George remained and held a steady job. Soon after John's return and his reunion with George, George began taking psychedelics and before long he too was using heroin. Both pursued their heroin careers together until they finally decided to leave the area, and both came to the West Coast. There they avoided heroin for a short while, but not very long afterward both were strung out again and were looking for help, this time with nowhere to run to.

They were living in the Haight-Ashbury neighborhood of San Francisco and knew of the clinic, but both were afraid of possible legal complications and therefore were hesitant about seeking help. Having heard that the clinic was a friendly, safe place to go, John eventually decided to give it a try. After a couple of months he managed to give up heroin and found a job in a restaurant. Two years later he was still doing well.

George never did come into the clinic and eventually returned to his Midwestern home town. Shortly thereafter he was arrested for possession of heroin for sale and is now serving a twenty-year sentence in the state penitentiary.

A community-based drug treatment and rehabilitation program like that of the Haight-Ashbury Free Medical Clinic may be viewed as a broadly based drug prevention program operating at all levels of drug abuse prevention. The different phases of drug prevention can be simply defined as follows:

1. *Primary Prevention:* Prevention of drug use in a previously uninvolved population.

2. *Secondary Prevention:* Prevention of the progression of drug abuse in an involved population that does not yet have any disability from its drug usage.

3. *Tertiary Prevention:* Rehabilitation of the drug-abusing population that has substantial residual disability as a result of its drug involvement.

Most rehabilitation programs operate in relative isolation and in effect only at the tertiary prevention level. To be most effective, a community-based drug rehabilitation organization like the Haight-Ashbury Free Medical Clinic must provide integrated services: i.e., it must offer primary, secondary, and tertiary preventive services simultaneously. These services include first: information, street-drug analysis, and alternative educational approaches; second: crisis intervention, detoxification, or ridding the body of the drugs, psychological counseling, and aftercare; third and finally: social and vocational rehabilitation for drug-involved individuals with substantial residual disability.

Of importance to primary prevention is the growing credibility crisis in the drug field in the United States. Much of this distrust has been produced by a dishonest and morally loaded approach to drug education on the part of America's dominant culture. The classic example is marijuana education, in which the Establishment has gone to extremes to substantiate scientifically invalid myths about cannabis: e.g., moderate consumption of marijuana leads to the use of harder drugs. Such myths have been disproven time and again by a variety of scientific bodies, including the National Commission on Marijuana and Drug Abuse. The propagation of such misinformation has created a "splatter effect" in which the potential consumer discovers that such information is dishonest and then refuses to believe any "official" drug information presented by the Establishment. Free clinics are widely accepted as credible sources of drug information.

The element of tertiary prevention is one of the greatest challenges facing the field of addiction today. American society has for a long time criminalized the addict and there is a great deal of prejudice against the individual who has a long history of compulsive drug involvement: "Once a junkie, always a junkie." As a consequence an individual whose life revolves around drugs finds that even when he or she becomes motivated and psychologically stable, it is impossible to get a job or escape any previous arrest record. Almost invariably the person returns either to dealing drugs to earn money, or to using drugs to escape the reality of this vicious cycle.

In the past few years society's concern about drug abuse has created one satisfying and acceptable alternative vocation for the addict: that of a recovered-addict counselor who helps other drug-involved individuals with their drug problems or works in community education programs. Of course, all addicts cannot become recovered-addict counselors, since funds are limited and since few recovered addicts (or anyone, for that matter) can cope with the extreme demands made upon drug counselors over prolonged periods of time.

Many other alternative industries and new vocational channels must be opened up for most of the addict population and at the same time the entire group, even those who are successful recovered-addict counselors, must learn new skills. One great concern at the Haight-Ashbury Free Clinic, where many of our employees are recovered-addicts or ex-drug abusers, is that if current support is suddenly cut off we would create another group of people prepared to work but not fitted for the job market: the only place for most of these suddenly unemployed staff members to go would be back on the street. Those recovered- or ex-addicts who are qualified and able must be strongly encouraged to participate in work-study programs, advance their education, and increase their vocational skills, particularly in the broader health-services area of which drug abuse counseling should be viewed as a subsegment. Certainly in the wider area of people service there will be many more vocational opportunities than just the recovered-addict counselor model. Such an expansive social and vocational rehabilitation program is tertiary prevention in its broadest sense.

A detailed description of the history of San Francisco's Haight-Ashbury Free Medical Clinic and its role in treating drug abuse problems is given in the book *Love Needs Care,* by this author and John Luce (see Suggestions for Further Reading). A list of each agent of abuse, with information such as short-term and long-term effects, potential for tolerance, physical dependence, and psychological dependence is given at the end of this book. I will now focus on individual major drugs of abuse with special discussions of new drug patterns that have appeared in recent years.

LSD

LSD was isolated from ergot, the product of a fungus that grows on rye and other grains, by Albert Hofmann, a chemist at the Sandoz Laboratory in Switzerland. In 1943 he accidentally ingested some of the substance and took the first "acid trip" in history, which he later vividly described.

LSD is an extremely potent substance, causing pharmacological effects in doses as low as ten to thirty micrograms (a microgram is a thousandth of a milligram, or a millionth of a gram). By weight it is about three million times as potent as crude marijuana.

People under the influence of LSD may have vivid alterations of their senses. There may be delusions of sight, or they may hear musical compositions they never heard before. Frequently there is a crossing of one sensory perception into another, called synesthesia. Music may be seen as colored lights, a pinprick becomes an explosion of lights, or twinkling lights become tinkling bells. The senses of time and space are distorted, often giving a feeling of timelessness and infinite space.

The basic distortion of perception may cause a loss of ability to discriminate self from outside objects. This may result in paranoia (exaggerated or unreal fears) or a mystical experience of "oneness" with the universe. Thus, rather than a frightening paranoia, a feeling of ecstasy or rapture may occur with a sense of complete identification with all things. Conversely, a complete sense of emptiness may result, with a sensation of death or nonexistence leading to a panic reaction or "bad trip."

Adverse reactions are greatly dependent on the mood of the individual, the setting in which the drug is taken, and the availability of someone to give support and reality orientation to avert bad trips.

Long-term LSD aftereffects—such as recurrence of drug-related symptoms with anxiety, paranoid feelings at times of stress, or visual recall reactions—commonly called flashbacks—may be seen. These generally fade away as the use of hallucinogens is discontinued. There have been many reports concerning the potential of

LSD to cause chromosomal breaks, perhaps leading to birth defects. As yet, these reports have not been proven. In the last few years there has been a gradual increase in the use of LSD after a decline in the early 1970s.

Long-term excessive use of LSD may produce personality changes toward passivity and nonviolence. The mass media called the passive youth "flower children" when they dominated Haight-Ashbury in its early days. However, after the flower children left, the major adolescent drug problem in the Haight-Ashbury district of San Francisco became amphetamines.

AMPHETAMINES

This class of drug was widely abused across the United States in the form of diet pills long before many of the '60s' young people were born. Amphetamines are potent central nervous system stimulants. Black market methamphetamine dominated the Haight-Ashbury and the high doses were commonly known as "speed." The "speed binge" can be divided into an action phase and a reaction phase.

During the action phase the user injects methamphetamine intravenously from one to ten times a day. With each injection the user experiences a "flash" that he or she describes as a "full-body orgasm." Between injections the user is euphoric (extremely elated), overactive, and overly excitable. This action phase may last for several days during which the individual does not sleep and rarely eats.

For a variety of reasons this action phase is terminated. The user may stop voluntarily because of fatigue; may become confused, paranoid, or panic-stricken and stop "shooting"; or he or she may simply run out of drugs. Whatever the reason for termination, the action phase is followed by the reaction phase in which the user goes rapidly from a very excitable state to one of extreme exhaustion. The "speed freak" may sleep for twenty-four to forty-eight hours and upon awakening is often quite hungry and may eat ravenously. Unfortunately, when food and sleep needs are satisfied, the user often enters a prolonged phase of extreme psychological depression. This depression is often so severe and intolerable that the user starts another speed binge and the cycle is repeated. A wide variety of medical complaints occur with continued use of intravenous methamphetamine at high doses. These include hepatitis, malnutrition, skin abscesses, and other medical problems.

The acute psychiatric problems seen with this drug pattern can be divided into four categories: the acute anxiety reaction, the psychotic reaction, the exhaustion reaction, and the withdrawal reaction.

Of the acute psychotic reactions, the amphetamine psychosis characterized by visual hallucinations, auditory hallucinations, and extreme paranoia represents the most dramatic and difficult. These paranoid characteristics may become so frightening to the speed freak that he or she may inject barbituates or heroin as a form of self-medication. Unfortunately, barbiturate and heroin dependence have resulted from this practice. The injecting of methamphetamine has decreased, but the abuse of stimulants continues as part of polydrug problems through all strata of society. Today we are seeing a dramatic rise in the use of yet another central nervous system stimulant, cocaine.

COCAINE

Cocaine is a potent central nervous system stimulant, and like any psychoactive drug, its pattern of use and abuse is strongly influenced by sociocultural factors including prevailing attitudes toward the drug. The general public has felt that cocaine was not particularly dangerous because it did not produce a well-defined physical dependency and abstinence syndrome, such as alcohol and heroin produce. However, when addiction is defined as compulsion, loss of control and continued use in spite of adverse consequences, cocaine drug hunger can be easily seen as an agent of addictive disease. Cocaine compulsion and drug hunger is probably the strongest of any drug, and produces a desire to continually reexperience the euphoria that cocaine can produce. The desired mood-altering effects of cocaine occur quickly and also disappear rapidly. This produces an immediate reward with a very rapid decline to the original feeling or, more likely a return to a feeling that is significantly less pleasurable than before the person began using the drug at that sitting. Thus a person can quickly become out of control in their desire to reexperience and maintain the euphoric "high," but because of blood saturation and other factors, this high is not able to be maintained, and the end result is a combination of anxiety and depression.

In the United States cocaine, an extract from the *Erythroxylon coca* leaf is usually "snorted" (inhaled through the nose). The more dangerous routes of administration, injection and smoking, produce a higher abuse potential. However, snorting cocaine can produce addiction rather easily. Although cocaine is classified as a narcotic *legally*, it has exactly the opposite pharmacological effect of the true narcotics such as heroin. Massive overdose with cocaine causes extreme *stimulation* of the central nervous system, producing severe anxiety, possible toxic cocaine psychosis and even convulsions. At higher doses of cocaine use, users can lose control and experience paranoid thinking and act upon such delusional thinking through violent acts, which the user will be amnesic to.

Because cocaine is such a potent central nervous system *stimulant*, most users will also use a central nervous system *depressant* such as alcohol, one of the most powerful depressants. Low level users will often have a glass of wine or beer to counteract the nervousness and anxiety that cocaine will produce. At higher levels of cocaine use, the user will need to use increasingly more depressants to counteract the much higher nervousness and anxiety. This "upper-downer" syndrome will produce a severe toll on the body of the user, and at higher doses can produce death by respiratory failure. Also, the effects of cocaine wear off much quicker than alcohol, for instance, and the user who has been using cocaine and alcohol will become a raging drunk as the effects of the cocaine wear off, but the alcohol remains active in the body.

STIMULANTS AND OTHER
SEDATIVE-HYPNOTICS

The barbiturates are general nervous system depressants prescribed by physicians for sedation and the induction of sleep. Many barbiturate preparations are available commercially. Barbiturate intoxication is quite similar to that obtained with ethyl alcohol (the type contained in liquor) and involves impairment of bodily motions, difficulty in thinking, slowness of comprehension and speech, emotional instability, and exaggeration of basic personality traits.

Repeated chronic intoxication with the barbiturates produces true physical dependence, and abrupt withdrawal of the drug from a dependent individual can produce severe and dangerous symptoms. When the drug use is stopped, the symptoms vary a great deal, depending on the duration and the amount of barbiturate used. Some patients experience only weakness and anxiety whereas others exhibit hallucinations, delirium, and convulsions. After approximately fifteen hours without the drug, a user's withdrawal symptoms begin to develop. They increase in magnitude, reaching a peak after thirty or forty hours. The progression of these withdrawal symptoms includes anxiety, muscle tremors, nausea, and occasional delirium with marked alterations in perception. Uncontrollable muscle twitches often herald the onset of a *grand mal* epileptic seizure.

As mentioned above, the intoxication with a short-acting barbiturate resembles that achieved with ethyl alcohol. Classically, individuals who abuse barbiturates are also those who are prone to abuse alcohol, and the same general psychiatric and social principles apply. During the summer of 1968 in Haight-Ashbury, however, new patterns of barbiturate abuse developed, which provided both challenging treatment situations and interesting drug correlates.

In 1968 the major adolescent drug problem in the San Francisco Bay Area was high-dose methamphetamine abuse. Prolonged central nervous system stimulation by this potent drug produces some very serious psychopathology. Typical symptoms are agitation and paranoia. Many young people, after being high on speed for long periods of time, began injecting secobarbital as the "downer," thereby temporarily relieving many of the symptoms of agitation and paranoia.

Unfortunately, much of this self-medication resulted in compulsive injection of secobarbital, with subsequent development of physical dependence, as the following case illustrates:

One summer, an eighteen-year-old white female came to the clinic in a state of acute anxiety. She had begun using methamphetamine one year previously and had been injecting the drug compulsively for six months. She described the gradual evolution of acute panic reactions, agitation, and paranoia. These psychiatric symptoms became so disturbing that when she was told "reds" (secobarbital) were a good downer she began injecting this drug. There was no flash—the orgasmic effect achieved by injecting methamphetamine—with reds, but she described a pleasurable euphoric rush. Of greater significance to her, the speed-induced psychiatric symptoms disappeared and she felt much better. She gradually increased her use of the intravenous barbiturates to a point where she felt "hooked" and uncomfortable. When she tried to stop the barbiturates she developed acute anxiety and came to the clinic in the early stages of barbiturate withdrawal.

Another sedative-hypnotic, or downer, that has gained great popularity among youth in the last few years is methaqualone, marketed by various United States drug companies under the names of Quaalude, Sopor, Somnafac, Optimil, and Parest. Unfortunately, the drug companies released this potent sedative-hypnotic to the American public before adequately testing it for abuse potential. In fact they vigorously advertised it as a drug free of the dangers of the barbiturates. Such promotional statements are simply not true, however, since methaqualone has overdose and addiction potential quite similar to the short-acting barbiturates, as shown in studies conducted by the Haight-Ashbury Free Medical Clinic and other drug treatment organizations. Youths describe methaqualone as the "love drug" because of its uninhibiting properties, and often mix it with alcohol, producing an added intoxication that is extremely dangerous and may produce death from severe respiratory depression.

Unfortunately, many young people also began injecting heroin as a downer for "speed runs." This, along with the abuse of several different drugs, provided a route to America's current, most serious illegal drug use problem among young people, namely heroin addiction.

HEROIN

In the late 1960s and the 1970s and continuing into the 1980s, heroin, a potent narcotic taken primarily by injection, moved out of the slums and ghettos to infect the sons and daughters of well-to-do citizens of middle-class America.

The alarm sounded across the country at that time did not emanate from concern about the long-standing drug abuse problems in racial ghettos, but rather was a result of "dope" reaching white youths in "good" neighborhoods.

Patterns of narcotic use dominant in the well-known drug communities of Greenwich Village in New York and the Haight-Ashbury district of San Francisco "rippled out" to other communities: Palo Alto, California; Ann Arbor, Michigan; Phoenix, Arizona; Grenell, Ohio; and Bar Harbor, Maine, are just a few.

The year 1971 became the year of the middle-class junkie. Shocked, distraught, unbelieving parents who discovered that their son or daughter was a heroin addict demanded government and community response to deal with the crisis.

Investigations revealed that young, teen-age white boys and girls, just like the boys and girls in the slums, rob, steal, and prostitute themselves, or "hustle," on the streets to support drug habits of $25, $50, and even $150 a day. For example, an eighteen-year-old son of a well-to-do California resident committed 376 burglaries of local homes to support his $150-a-day habit, which required that he steal and "fence" $500 to $600 worth of merchandise a day.

Selling drugs to friends in school is another way young people finance a drug habit. In some schools, the lavatory is called "the drugstore" because of the volume of illicit business done between classes. The "new breed" of heroin addicts marks a drastic phase in youthful drug abuse.

Police in most of the larger cities generally agree that almost 50 percent of all property crimes are committed by young heroin addicts desperate to get enough cash together to make their "connection." The classic "nickel bag" of heroin is a plastic bag or rubber balloon that sells on the street for five to fifteen dollars. It contains about 3 percent heroin, bulked up with milk sugar, quinine, or any other white, crystalline powder additive that looks like heroin. This might also be household cleanser or strychnine. The nickel bag is no longer the exclusive merchandise of the ghetto dweller.

Ghetto youths, blacks, Mexican-Americans, and Puerto Ricans, some minority leaders feel, have too long been prey for rich, white drug pushers who have exploited them with diluted dope. Ghetto dwellers bought heroin to diminish the acute pain of living in an almost escape-proof trap of poverty, racism, and despair. They came to see long-standing traffic in heroin as a conspiracy by whites to keep them dependent and "nodding on the street corner" instead of militantly organizing for their rights.

Although not the most chemically destructive of the currently abused drugs (sedative-hypnotics cause more severe addictions, and amphetamines in high doses are more acutely destructive to the body and mind), heroin provides the worst compulsive drug-use pattern. Once you are "on it" you crave it and even hunger for "garbage" heroin, which has been cut or diluted by a dozen or more middlemen. Unless a person is independently wealthy he or she has to steal or hustle in some illegal way. Typically this means that a user's whole life is involved in a criminal world. Although the popular "stepping-stone" theory that marijuana smoking leads to heroin addiction has been discredited by most analytical people, there is substance in the contention that people introduced into an illegal criminal underground to buy or sell one drug will soon be exposed to the opportunity to try others, heroin included.

Many converts to heroin over the last decade might never have gotten started had there not been powerful external social pressures for them to do so. Heroin use to many, however, seems almost a death wish. Perhaps it is even a symbolic substitution for suicide. The new-style heroin users are sick because their lives and their world, despite affluence, are sick. They are almost totally alienated from the rest of America. They no longer identify with or trust society, or even see much good in it. They feel that they have been betrayed by their parents, their teachers, and their society, so they drop out—often literally. Heroin, they believe, is their best, or perhaps only, path for escape.

There are, of course, some predisposing factors to heroin dependence. Some users, even from childhood, have a serious and well-established personality pathology, often caused by psychological injury, unhappiness, violence, neglect in the home, or socioeconomic deprivation.

Some types of treatment of heroin addicts are discussed later in this book, and fortunately treatment of the addict using a variey of therapeutic approaches is gaining more public support. As a consequence of this changing public attitude and increased financial support for education, research, and treatment, as well as a more balanced law enforcement approach toward the control of the distribution and supply of heroin, 1973 saw for the first time a decrease in the nationwide heroin epidemic, and it appeared that we had turned the corner on this particular aspect of the nation's drug problem. However, this relief was short-lived. Drug epidemiologists have since recognized an ongoing long-term cycle of heroin abuse that is periodically affected by world events. For example, troubles in the Middle East have brought the availability of over 90 percent pure Iranian heroin. This potent drug is smoked in the same circles as "free base" cocaine by people who sincerely believe that they are not becoming heroin addicts.

DESIGNER DRUGS

Starting in the late 1970s with the advent of Alpha Methyl Phentanyl, an analogue of the powerful pain killer fentanyl used in hospitals for operative pain, a new drug scourge has spread into the streets of America. A doctor at the University of California Medical School at Davis coined the term "designer drugs" for these substances. They are synthesized by illicit chemists devising formulas that retain a drug's mind-affecting qualities but change the chemical structure sufficiently to escape prosecution under current drug laws.

The fentanyl drugs are like heroin but much more

powerful, increasing the danger of overdose deaths among their users. Another designer drug, MPPP, which resembles the prescription pain killer Demerol^R, or meperidine, often contains an impurity that causes permanent paralysis. This state, which resembles the effects of Parkinson's disease, is caused by the destruction of brain cells.

Other designer drugs include substances that resemble the dangerous psychedelic phencyclidine or PCP, known on the street as "Angel Dust."

The appearance of these drugs indicates that underground chemists who manufacture drugs for the illicit market have become increasingly sophisticated and are becoming capable of synthesizing a wide range of previously unknown substances. These drugs are a potential regulatory and enforcement nightmare in that, theoretically, if heroin-like drugs, or other substances resembling other scheduled substances can be made anywhere, any time, at will, there may be no effective way of stopping them. Such a prospect makes primary prevention and drug education for the young more important than ever.

One drug group that is often connected with designer drugs is the methoxylated amphetamines. This group includes MDMA, known generally as Ecstasy or Adam, a drug that was actually synthesized in 1914. MDMA was banned in 1985 as a dangerous substance, but has been the center of a controversy between scientists and doctors who maintain that it may have medical usefulness in psychiatric treatment and the Drug Enforcement Administration that feels its dangers outweigh keeping it available for research.

POLYDRUG ABUSE

The broader problem of drug abuse continues to be a substantial one and the new trend is toward the multiple use of the drugs described in this and other chapters in this book.

This new drug phase has been described as polydrug abuse. More and more we are seeing individuals abusing combinations of barbituates and heroin, amphetamines and barbiturates, and barbiturates and/or methaqualone and alcohol. This growing trend toward polydrug abuse presents substantial new challenges to drug treatment programs, for multiple drug abuse cannot be handled with drug maintenance approaches such as methadone maintenance and needs the integrated services of crisis intervention, detoxification, psychological aftercare, and social and vocational rehabilitation at the community level to be truly effective. In addition, there needs to be more stress on drug prevention and on finding alternatives to the dominant-culture philosophy of "better living through chemistry" and "a pill for all ills."

Fortunately the dominant culture in the United States is gradually accepting a combined social and health-care model regarding the use of drugs, and, with the exception of some misplaced lapses into hysteria, is putting in perspective the prevailing criminal-punishment rationale for the illegal drug user. In addition, one of the most encouraging signs that I have seen when traveling across the United States is the growing attempt by young people to understand themselves and realize their hopes and potentials by seeking alternatives to the pressures placed upon them to use and abuse both illegal *and* legal psychoactive drugs. Much greater emphasis should be placed on helping this self-realization and alternative models so that young people can more and more make an informed, individual, and responsible decision as to what they want to do with their bodies and minds.

RECOVERY

The most important aspect of drug use and addiction is the fact that recovery from addiction is possible. This fact is certainly a highest of priorities relative to addiction among contemporary youth. There have been many responses to the treatment of addiction, and the state of the art knowledge in this field points to the use of chemical dependency units for the medical and psychological management of the addiction and growth-oriented support groups for the recovery from drug addiction.

Addiction to powerful central nervous system effective drugs impacts on the youth's mental, emotional, spiritual, social, financial and physical lives. Inpatient chemical dependency units address these issues directly. Typically such a unit in a hospital will recommend a minimum stay of about 3–4 weeks which is just enough time for the person to understand the severity of chemical addiction and learn appropriate skills that will allow reentry into society without the use of drugs. These chemical dependency units will lay the foundation for the reentry back into society, including the numerous family issues which predated the addiction and those which occurred as a result. But such treatment is only the first step in a life of recovery from drug abuse. The various self-help groups such as Alcoholics Anonymous, Narcotics Anonymous, Cocaine Anonymous, Alateen and Al-Anon are perhaps the most powerful community resources available. These self-help groups help the person to talk with others about their chemical dependency, continue learning about addiction, learn further skills at saying "no" to drugs and help them to address their own personal, emotional and spiritual growth. These groups and others, such as Teens Kick-Off (TKO) in San Francisco specifically address chemical dependency as it effects the person, their family and especially youth.

COCAINE

Margaret O. Hyde

Cocaine may be the most powerful drug in the world and one of the most popular. Certainly, its abuse has increased dramatically in recent years and so has the information about the effect of cocaine on the human body. Not all users exhibit debilitating physical and behavioral problems, so some users assume that cocaine can be used safely. Drs. Arnold M. Washton, Mark S. Gold, and A.L.C. Pottash, who have studied numerous cocaine users, note that the drug seems to have a subtle ability to delude the user into thinking that its intake is not problem producing. Rehabilitation experts, emergency room personnel, and medical examiners have a far different opinion. Cheaper cocaine and a simpler way to obtain the pure form make it even easier to "overdose dead on cocaine."

A new form of cocaine known as "crack" has appeared on the streets. Crack is a more powerful and more addicting form than cocaine hydrochloride, the common form known as "snow," "coke," etc. High school students have been known to become almost instantaneously addicted to crack, the pure cocaine crystals that look like small beige "rocks" and are marketed illegally in transparent vials that resemble large vitamin capsules. "Crack It Up," "Buy One, Get One Free" are common business slogans for dealers, some of whom have been seen standing on the streets cracking imaginary whips to signal what they have to sell. In some cities, crack is sold in candy stores and school corridors. In suburban communities, dealers, who are usually users, are more apt to make sales at social functions. Some experts fear that the baby boom of the 1960s has shifted from marijuana to cocaine.

Crack is popular among adolescents, relatively inexpensive, and the cause of an alarming increase in the number of people seeking treatment for physical and emotional problems. Users can be rendered completely dysfunctional in a two- or three-month period. Kate was one of these people.

At the age of 17, Kate was in the top quarter of her class in a suburban high school where most of the students were making plans for college. Kate knew that she needed a scholarship and she was working very hard to increase her grade average. She often felt that the situation was hopeless; she would never be good enough to get a scholarship in a college that was prestigious enough to make her parents happy.

Kate's friend, Bill, encouraged her to relax. He and Kate often smoked marijuana, but Kate considered giving up all parties and concentrating on the school activities that would look good on her college applications. Bill told her he had a better idea. He had just tried cocaine, and he was sure that cocaine would boost Kate's self-confidence.

Kate hesitated when Bill offered to introduce her to cocaine. She had heard terrible stories about people who got so involved with the drug that they spent all their money on it. She had read about a boy who had died when using cocaine. Bill assured her that a few snorts would not hurt her, and it might be just what she needed to pick her up. Bill took her to a party where friends were snorting lines of cocaine through rolled hundred dollar bills.

At first, Kate decided that snorting cocaine just wasn't worth the money, but when she tried crack, she decided it was the most wonderful feeling in the world. She was enveloped with a sense of well-being, and she felt she could conquer any obstacle. She felt exhilarated, strong, and very self-confident. Nothing could stop her from doing everything she wanted to do. She had reached the ultimate high. The feeling did not last long. She felt depressed, lost her energy, and was told she had "crashed."

Kate noticed that some of the people at the party were involved in a variety of sexual activities. Many women were selling favors in order to get money for more cocaine. Some otherwise distinguished-looking people were begging others for more cocaine, promising anything to get more crack. The suppliers, coke abusers themselves, took in large amounts of cash, then left to get a new supply of crack. Some women sold their jewelry; men and women made out large checks and continued to do crack until their money ran out. Many seemed to be doing crack nonstop. One woman acted almost as if her mind was burned out. Bill told Kate not to pay any attention to her, but Kate felt very let down and frightened when her high wore off. She persuaded Bill to leave with her, but she knew she would go back again. Maybe she and Bill would just fool around with cocaine once in a while. They would be different from those crazy people who spent all their money on it. They would be sensible about their use of cocaine.

After a few more experiences, Kate and Bill could barely wait till they managed to get enough money to go to a crack house, a place where people gathered for binges that lasted several days. Kate gave up her idea of going to college. She left home when her parents tried to talk to her about what they considered her problem. To Kate, the only problem was getting enough money to buy more cocaine. She was on a roller coaster of highs and depressions.

Kate is just one of a growing number of young people who are big-time losers in the cocaine epidemic. Kate is working out her problem in a rehabilitation center. Bill was not so lucky. One night when Bill was using cocaine, he went to the bedroom to lie down for a while on the waterbed. He had a small seizure, got up, snorted some more cocaine, and went back to the bed. Soon he suffered such violent seizures that friends could not hold him. He died of respiratory collapse.

Although the pattern of cocaine use is changing today, it remained the same for about 4,700 years. Cocaine is derived from the waxy leaves of a tropical shrub called *Erythroxylon coca* (not the same as the cacao plant that bears chocolate beans) and for thousands of years, the cocaine remained hidden in its leaves. The bitterness, numbing, and psychoactive properties protected it from insects and foraging animals. People used the leaves in religious, magical, medical, and recreational contexts as long ago as 3000 B.C. Leaves were chewed whole or in powdered form, swallowed in combination with other ingredients, and/or smoked with or without tobacco.

Coca was introduced in Europe about 1580, and it eventually found its way into a variety of products, including drugs for medical use, wines, lozenges, cigars, cigarettes, and even in chewing gum. Doctors became enthusiastic about cocaine as a drug after its isolation by chemists between 1855 and 1860. Along with the introduction of the name, cocaine, in 1859/1860 came a new popularity. Medical doctors increased their use of the drug, patent medicine manufacturers exploited it, and people used it casually for its euphoric properties. Cocaine appeared in flake crystals, tablets, and solutions for injection, ointments, and nasal sprays. A variety of soft drinks included coca and cocaine, Coca Cola being the most popular. (Cocaine was removed from Coca Cola about 1903.)

In the period between 1860 and the early twentieth century, uncontrollable addiction, adverse physical effects, and other problems associated with cocaine use were noted in both medical and lay articles. By 1914, its manufacture, possession, sale, distribution, and use were placed under legal control. Both medical and nonmedical use declined in the next decades, and interest in cocaine seemed to wane.

In the early 1970s, cocaine use again became a recreational drug of choice, and at that time it was generally considered to be a "safe recreational drug." Although there were experiments with new preparations and patterns of use, most cocaine was taken into the body through the nose. Some users injected cocaine directly into the bloodstream. Studies at this time indicated the tendency of users to increase the dosage and to suffer many adverse reactions.

Today, cocaine is generally sniffed once by those who want to experiment, or on occasion by recreational users in social situations. Some of the recreational users do not realize that they are on their way to becoming compulsive users, one of those who have lost control over their cocaine habit and who sniff, shoot intravenously, or smoke whenever they can. They shift rapidly from ecstacy to misery, and they stop only when they run out of cocaine, are exhausted physically, or run into some physical complication that prevents them from continuing.

By the mid-1970s, compulsive users began appearing in medical clinics and chronic cocaine abuse was commonly associated with psychological dependence, depression on withdrawal, and sleep disturbances. Researchers found that in heavy users, euphoria was often counterbalanced by adverse reactions such as tension, anxiety, paranoia, hallucinations, and sometimes overdose and death.

At the beginning of the 1980s, smoking coca paste and cocaine free-basing became increasingly popular. In the countries where coca plants grow, the leaves are steeped with kerosene, sulfuric acid, and an alkali. This forms coca paste. When hydrochloric acid is added, cocaine hydrochloride, the form most commonly sold in the United States, is formed. Dealers cut this cocaine to stretch their profits, using a variety of materials such as amphetamine, procaine, lidocaine, quinine, and sugar. The cocaine sold on the street may be cut so much that it contains no cocaine at all.

Both crude paste and cocaine hydrochloride are transported illegally from South American countries and distributed to the dealers. The first reports of coca paste smoking came from Peru and were followed by reports from some other South American countries and of sporadic instances in the United States. Coca paste is usually smoked after it is sprinkled on tobacco or marijuana. Although smoking coca paste is a relatively cheap way of obtaining a brief ecstatic state, reports of the fairly frequent appearance of psychotic reactions that come with chronic use deter some who consider it. According to Dr. Sydney Cohen, author of four books and hundreds of articles on the subject of psychopharmacology and drug abuse, both coca paste smoking and intravenous injections of cocaine lead to the paranoid state more frequently than when equivalent amounts are inhaled.

Intravenous injections of cocaine are believed to have greatly decreased because users fear contracting AIDS (Acquired Immune Deficiency Syndrome) through this method. Free-basing appears to be on the decline for a different reason. Cocaine free base is commonly made by the user with a kit that converts cocaine hydrochloride to basic cocaine. This product is more volatile than the more common form and readily passes into the fumes from the pipe in which it is heated. Accidents resulting from the preparation of free base, and the lighting of the metal pipe by people under the influence of drugs are common and sometimes fatal. When smoked, the potent cocaine base is rapidly absorbed in the lungs and carried to the brain in a few seconds, causing an intense but short-lived high. This is followed by a depression and aggravated drug craving.

People who free-base have been known to develop tolerance to cocaine, with estimates that they may be doing enough coke in one day to kill a dozen nonusers. In addition to tolerance, there appears to be a physical withdrawal in some heavy users, a deep depression that can last for weeks.

Crack, the form of cocaine described at the beginning of this chapter, is the equivalent of free base, but it is safer than making it with a kit and often cheaper. However, crack is far from safe. There is the risk of unpredictable medical complications, including seizures and death.

Cocaine has been called a random killer. Dr. Mark Gold, director of Fair Oaks Hospital in New Jersey, notes that there is no way of telling who will die from cocaine and who won't. It might be a regular user or a first-time user. Death may come from a variety of causes, such as respiratory failure, cerebral hemorrhage, an allergy to cocaine or the material used to cut it, irregular heart beat and cardiac arrest.

An estimated million people in the United States are believed to be profoundly dependent on cocaine, and the true number may be far higher. Calls to the national cocaine helpline, 800-COCAINE, continue to increase. Anyone who is concerned about a possible problem with cocaine may call this helpline free of charge.

The slogan, SPEED KILLS, helped to curb the abuse of amphetamines during the sixties. Today many young people are spreading the slogan, COCAINE KILLS.

MARIJUANA

William H. McGlothlin, Ph.D.
(updated by Margaret O. Hyde)

Dr. McGlothlin is well known for his investigations, consultations, and writing in connection with marijuana. He was a consultant to the National Marijuana Commission in the United States and to the World Health Organization.

DESCRIPTION AND HISTORY

Marijuana is one of the oldest and most widely used mind-altering drugs known. The Chinese described it in their literature almost 5,000 years ago. The United Nations estimates that there are some two hundred million users throughout the world. It is the second most popular intoxicant in the world—alcohol being the first.

Marijuana (also known as "grass" and "pot") comes from a tall gangly plant whose scientific name is *Cannabis sativa,* or simply cannabis. The plant grows wild in most parts of the world and is cultivated for the drug in some Eastern countries. The stem of the plant contains a tough fiber, which has long been used to manufacture hemp rope and crude cloth; hence it is also known as the hemp plant. The seeds are used in birdseed mixtures. Most of the drug is contained in the resin secreted around the flower, seeds, and topmost leaves. Like the date palm, an individual cannabis plant is either male or female, and until recently, it was thought that only the female plant produced the drug. It is now known that both male and female plants contain the drug; however, since the female bloom is larger than the male, the female does produce more of the drug. Marijuana, as it is normally sold, consists of the dried leaves, seeds and small stems of either cultivated or wild plants. Seeds and stems are removed (manicured) prior to use. The potency of marijuana depends on the content of the principal active chemical, delta-9 tetrahydrocannabinol (THC). This, in turn, depends on the variety of the cannabis plant, when it is harvested, and the portions of the plant included in the material. The amount of THC also depends on the age and conditions of storage. Much of the marijuana available today is ten to fifteen times stronger, and therefore more harmful, than it was in the 1960s and 1970s.

In India and other Eastern countries, where cannabis is cultivated for the drug, much more potent preparations are obtained. The strongest of these is hashish, which consists of pure resin. Hashish is generally stronger than marijuana, although it is subject to deterioration with age and may be relatively weak after long periods of storage. It is important to distinguish between various potencies, because, like beer and distilled liquor, the stronger preparations have a greater capacity for abuse than do the weaker forms of the drug.

Cannabis has a long and varied history in India and other Middle Eastern countries. It has been used for thousands of years in medicines prescribed to relieve pain, tension, and various physical ailments. Cannabis also has had a prominent role in religious practices, especially in India, being used to enhance meditation and mystical trances. Finally, it has had widespread use as a euphoriant (a producer of euphoria, a feeling of well-being) or as an intoxicant, much as alcohol is used in this country. The majority of people using the drug for this purpose do so in moderation, but some take it regularly in large amounts, resulting in a state similar to alcoholism. Excessive amounts of the drug are more easily consumed when the stronger or more potent preparations, such as hashish, are used. Tolerance to hashish develops at a moderate rate, so the regular user needs larger doses to achieve the same "high."

From India, the use of cannabis spread to other parts of the world. It was introduced into Europe about 1850, but its use there was very rare up until the last few years. Marijuana has a fairly long history of use in Mexico and Latin America, and it was introduced into the United States around 1910 by Mexican laborers.

The spread of marijuana in this country was very largely confined to lower socioeconomic minority groups until around 1960, when its use among students and other young people began to increase.

PHYSICAL AND MENTAL EFFECTS

The effects of marijuana depend on the potency of the preparation and the amount consumed. They range from effects so slight and subtle that an inexperienced user is unable to detect them, to dramatic alterations of consciousness that approach the effects of LSD, mescaline, psilocybin, and the other strong hallucinogens. Hallucinogens are drugs that produce hallucinations, or more accurately, illusions or waking dreams. Marijuana belongs to the family of hallucinogenic drugs, but its effects are usually much milder than those of LSD. More dramatic effects are generally associated with the use of hashish.

Marijuana is generally smoked. The smoke is deeply inhaled and then held in the lungs until it is absorbed. Marijuana may also be ingested in the form of a drink, cakes, or other food. When smoked, the effects are almost immediate and last from one to three hours. When consumed in foods or beverages, the effects begin in one-half to one hour and last about four hours. The length of action is longer for larger amounts consumed.

The immediate physiological effects are rather minimal. The most consistent effects are a rise in pulse rate and a reddening of the eyes. Early reports indicated that the pupils of the eyes become larger, but this has been found to be incorrect. There is often a greater frequency of urination. Hunger may increase, especially for sweets. With larger doses, there is a dryness of the mouth and throat and a sensation of dizziness.

There is also a decrease in ability to perform physical tasks requiring muscular coordination. Perception of time and distance is distorted, and thought processes are impaired. These effects are greater for large doses and are more pronounced for inexperienced users.

Of course, the principal reason for taking marijuana is its emotional effect. This is generally described as being "high," which consists of a feeling of well-being, relaxation, euphoria, freedom from anxiety, and reduced inhibition. Enjoyment of music is enhanced; the subjective senses of taste and touch are keener. Marijuana is most often taken in a small social group, and a feeling of emotional closeness with other members of the group is frequently reported. The effects normally end in drowsiness and sleep.

With larger doses, or in highly susceptible individuals, the user may experience perceptual changes, body distortions, feelings of being separated from one's body, and dramatic waking dreams or fantasies somewhat similar to those resulting from LSD. These effects may be frightening and can result in panic or, on rare occasions, even in temporary psychotic reactions,[1] especially if the user is inexperienced or takes the drug in an insecure setting. Such a person may become suspicious or paranoid. He may also be convinced he will not return to normal.

THE CONTROVERSY

The above description of marijuana, its history, and its immediate effects are facts about which there is little disagreement. However, when we discuss whether or not its use is harmful to the individual and society, we are immediately involved in cultural taboos, questions of morality, and other controversial issues about which there is a great deal of disagreement. As every student knows, many people currently are questioning the arguments that have been used to justify the harsh legal

[1] A psychotic reaction and psychosis are technically correct terms for what many people refer to as losing one's mind, becoming insane, or having a nervous breakdown.

penalties sometimes imposed on marijuana users. Questions are asked, such as: "Even if it is harmful to the individual, doesn't a person have a right to use it as long as he doesn't harm others?" "Does it make sense to put one person in jail for using marijuana and at the same time encourage the use of another intoxicant, alcohol, by means of widespread advertising?" These are very real and also very complex issues. They tend to cloud any objective discussion of what is known about the harm or lack of harm resulting from marijuana use. For this reason, I propose to set aside these aspects of the question, and also to ignore temporarily the very real consequences of violating the present marijuana laws.

Suppose marijuana use were not illegal. What questions would a rational person then ask in deciding whether or not to use it? She or he would probably ask whether it is physically or mentally harmful; whether it is addicting or habituating, or might interfere with other aspects of his or her life in some way; whether its use might lead to use of more harmful drugs or to other undesirable forms of behavior, and how these relate to the age of the user, the frequency of use, and the amount consumed. From a positive standpoint, one might also ask what benefits, if any, could be attained through its use. In the following discussion, I shall attempt to provide the available factual information on these questions, independent of cultural and moral issues.

Is marijuana physically harmful?

In spite of considerable research on marijuana, today's knowledge has been compared with the state of knowledge about alcohol one hundred years ago and that of tobacco fifty years ago. Most of the information on marijuana's effects on the body has been established through studies on both humans and animals, but some is based only on research animals. Stringent United States drug-testing laws require that most research be conducted on men over 18 years of age. Very few studies have involved women or adolescents.

One of the concerns about the physical effects of marijuana is the length of time that marijuana stays in the body. When marijuana is smoked, THC, its active ingredient, is absorbed by many tissues and organs. The body transforms THC into metabolites which can be detected in the urine and blood of humans up to a week after marijuana has been smoked. Storage of fat-soluble THC in organs such as lungs, brain, and the reproductive system has created concern in many researchers.

To date, no definitive neurological study of humans has turned up evidence of marijuana-related permanent brain damage, but there is considerable debate about the effects of marijuana on the brain. Some researchers claim that long-term changes occur in brain wave patterns, and these claims are being further investigated. In a study of rhesus monkeys, the animals were trained to smoke a marijuana cigarette five days a week for six months. The researcher reported that persistant changes in the structure of the monkey's brain cells followed. More research is being done in this area.

There is no evidence that use of marijuana produces any direct organic brain damage, but, again, there is insufficient evidence to rule out the possibility that prolonged, heavy use produces such damage. We do know that rather gross personality changes sometimes accompany such use, and this type of change could be related to physical changes in the brain.

As previously mentioned, marijuana-induced panic reactions are not uncommon among inexperienced users. On rare occasions, these reactions may precipitate a temporary psychosis. These psychotic episodes usually clear up within a few hours or days but some have been known to last for longer periods of time. Almost all authorities in this country agree that marijuana will not produce a lasting psychosis in an otherwise stable person. Whereas hospital admissions for LSD-induced psychosis have been quite frequent in recent years, cases related to marijuana use are rare.

Marijuana contains many of the cancer-causing chemicals and lung irritants found in tobacco smoke and some unique to the marijuana plant. Although more tobacco cigarettes may be smoked, marijuana smokers inhale the smoke very deeply into their lungs and hold it there to get full effects of the drug, resulting in long exposure to harmful chemicals. One cancer-causing agent is 70 percent more abundant in marijuana smoke than in tobacco smoke. There is also more tar. According to the American Lung Association, regular marijuana smokers increase their risk of developing lung cancer, emphysema, bronchitis, and other respiratory ailments.

Controversy continues about the harmful effects on the immune and reproductive systems. Chronic use decreases male sex drive, interest, and male sexual hormone levels, and can interfere with the menstrual cycle in women. There is evidence that marijuana may be hazardous for those with heart disorder because the drug increases the heart rate. There is also limited evidence that unborn babies may be harmed by marijuana, and that it would be unwise for pregnant women to use the drug. The same is true with respect to tobacco and alcohol.

Is marijuana addicting?

Much of the confusion about this question has resulted from a very loose use of words combined with the emotional climate surrounding the illegal use of drugs. Both the public and law enforcement agencies often incorrectly lump all these drugs together under the label "narcotics," which implies they are addicting. People who attempt to describe drug effects objectively apply the term "addictive" only to drugs that cause physical withdrawal symptoms when they are discontinued after a period of habitual use and that produce a tolerance in the body, i.e., a condition in which the person requires increasingly higher doses to attain the same effect. Drugs clearly falling under this definition are heroin and the other opiates, and the barbiturates. Alcohol used very heavily also qualifies under this definition.

A little reflection will demonstrate the difficulty resulting from attaching emotional and moral judgments to words, even words precisely defined, as in this case. For instance, heavy use of tobacco produces very clear physical withdrawal symptoms, and even the habitual coffee drinker is often pretty irritable if he misses his morning caffeine; yet we would not consider these people addicts in the usual sense of the term.

When we move from addiction to terms such as "habit-forming" or "psychological dependence"[2] we have a great deal more trouble with definitions. It is clear that anyone may be psychologically dependent on almost any form of behavior that he or she enjoys, whether it is reading murder mysteries, surfing, watching television, or playing bridge. Whether or not psychological dependence is harmful depends on the consequences of the behavior rather than the existence of such behavior.

Now, as for the question of whether marijuana is addicting, we can definitely conclude that it is not. The daily marijuana user will experience less physical discomfort on being deprived of the drug than will the regular smoker of tobacco cigarettes. Also, with continued use there is little necessity to increase the dose of marijuana, although there is some evidence of tolerance to the effects among frequent users. Studies of heavy users in this country, and among chronic hashish smokers in Eastern countries, report that users experience some irritation when the drug is withdrawn, but the symptoms are so mild as to be easily ignored. There is definitely no compulsion to obtain the drug, as in the case of heroin users.

Regarding psychological dependency, the majority of people who use marijuana do so occasionally for recreational purposes in somewhat the same way that the moderate users of alcohol have a few drinks now and

[2] Psychological dependence means that although the user does not physically crave a particular drug, emotionally he feels he must have it.

then. Neither group could be considered psychologically dependent on a drug. For a minority, however, marijuana use plays a more important role and occupies an integral or central part in their daily lives. This group, known as "potheads," is psychologically dependent on the drug. Whether their behavior is harmful to them is the next question.

Does prolonged use of marijuana result in personality change?

A number of authors have attributed subtle personality and behavior changes to the frequent use of marijuana, especially among adolescents. In particular, a passive or "amotivational syndrome" has been described in which the frequent user tends to lose interest in school, work, or other long-term goals. These reported effects are difficult to prove or refute because there are other important factors involved. The fact that heavy marijuana users characteristically exhibit certain traits does not necessarily mean that they are caused by the drug use. Such traits may tend to be already present in people who elect to use marijuana in this manner.

Nevertheless, it does appear that marijuana use significantly contributes to the attitudes and behavior of the pothead, i.e., the person who uses marijuana very frequently and who has made the drug an important part of his life. Some observers have reported that the drug exerts a chronic tranquilizing or depressant effect, and that reversals in mood and behavior are evident a few weeks after discontinuing its use. It is known that marijuana intoxication produces heightened suggestibility, which likely makes the user more amenable to adopting the attitudes and values of the subculture in which the drug is taken. Finally, it may be that an impressionable young person who is chronically exposed to the state of marijuana intoxication simply learns to think in a similar manner when not intoxicated.

Regardless of the issue of how much, and in what manner marijuana is responsible for personality change, it is clear that the pothead often exhibits a fairly well-defined set of characteristics. He or she tends to drift along with little concern for adjustment to anything other than immediate needs and impulses. Failure to attain the goals of society, parents, or self is resolved by a denial of their validity or desirability. The pothead also tends to exhibit a characteristic looseness in his or her thinking. He or she adopts primitive, magical explanations of events and relations as opposed to rational, factually determined thinking. In general, there is a tendency to retreat to a rather naive and childish world, which leaves him or her poorly equipped to cope with external reality.

These observations are not intended as an indictment of the pothead in terms of the cultural value system, but rather are made from the standpoint of individual adjustment. No amount of denial of an outside reality can remove an individual entirely from the demands of his environment. Ignoring basic health practices will result in illness. Failure to come to terms with the basic economic demands of holding a job will produce conflict with society. Substitution of magical thinking for rationality takes away a human being's most powerful tool, the ability to think logically. And failure to develop a discipline for expressing oneself prevents one from obtaining those major satisfactions available from individual accomplishment.

Does marijuana lead to the use of other, more harmful drugs?

One of the major arguments that was long used to support the suppression of marijuana was that its use was a stepping-stone to heroin use. According to this view, the pleasure associated with marijuana becomes less satisfying with continued use, and the person then seeks greater kicks in heroin. Those who believe this explanation cite as evidence the fact that the large marjority of heroin addicts previously have used marijuana. Those who deny the accuracy of this explanation argue that although many heroin addicts have also used marijuana, this fact does not mean that one behavior *causes* the other, any more than the prior use of alcohol causes heroin use. They cite the fact that only a small percentage of today's marijuana users have ever tried heroin, and the occurrence of heroin addiction among middle-class students is relatively rare.

Observations of the current drug usage among young people reveal that both of these arguments are partly right and partly wrong. If the person from whom one buys marijuana also sells heroin, and if in the process of using marijuana one is placed in contact with other people who use heroin, then obviously the use of marijuana increases the opportunity for initiation to heroin. Several years ago, when marijuana use was limited mostly to lower socioeconomic groups, being a marijuana user often afforded the opportunity to obtain and use heroin. Now, of course, many young persons use marijuana fairly frequently without ever having seen heroin. On the other hand, heavy involvement in the current drug subculture will often provide access to heroin along with a variety of other drugs.

While progression from marijuana to heroin use is relatively rare among middle-class youth, it is well established that the use of marijuana does play a role in the initiation to the more potent and dangerous hallucinogens, such as LSD and PCP. A number of surveys have found that the majority of students who use marijuana several times a week have also used hallucinogens. Experimentation with the more destructive drugs does not seem to be caused by an ever-increasing need for greater kicks as much as by a lack of rationality. As discussed in the previous section, the chronic marijuana user often is concerned only with experiences of the present and appears to deny or ignore the future consequences of his or her behavior, even though it may be highly destructive. This sometimes leads to a willingness to try any available drug without questioning the possible effects. To the extent that heavy marijuana use contributes to this lack of restraint and unrealistic behavior, it must share the blame for these dangerous practices with respect to other drugs.

Finally, there is the question of whether marijuana use is likely to lead to use of the more potent preparations of the drug, such as hashish. In cultures where the drug has been used for centuries, the average daily amount consumed is much larger than in the U.S. One likely reason for this is that the use of hashish or other potent preparations in these countries makes it easier to smoke more of the active ingredient. Some years ago the marijuana available in the United States was of relatively low potency—generally less than 1 percent THC—and the amount of THC consumed was almost trivial in comparison to that of users in countries such as India, Egypt, Greece, and Jamaica. At that time it was speculated that if hashish, or the even more concentrated extract (called hashish oil) became generally available, the very heavy patterns of use observed in Eastern countries might occur here. Hashish and hashish oil are now available to some extent; but more commonly, it is the high-potency marijuana containing 3 to 10 percent THC that makes it feasible to consume large amounts of the active ingredient.[3] Marijuana of this potency is quite expensive, but has become fairly widely available in recent years. People smoking several of these high-potency cigarettes per day are consuming amounts of THC comparable to that of users in traditional hashish cultures. Most marijuana smokers in the U.S. do not seem to be motivated to take the drug in these large amounts. Recent surveys show the percentage of high school seniors using it daily halved over a seven-year period. In 1978, 11 percent reported daily use, while in 1984, the percentage dropped to 5 percent. Occasional use dropped by a third during that period.

[3] It should be noted that while substances alleged to be THC are frequently sold on the illegal market, they are always fraudulent. THC is very difficult to manufacture and is never available on the illicit market. Frequently drugs sold as THC are actually PCP.

Does marijuana lead to crime?

The claim that marijuana leads to criminal behavior (other than its use) has been largely discounted, although this argument was frequently advanced until the last few years. It was argued that: (1) the user may commit acts of violence in a marijuana-induced state of panic or psychosis; (2) heavy use causes theft and other minor criminal behavior as a result of a decline in moral discipline in the user and the loss of legitimate earnings due to a drug-induced lethargy; and (3) its use was said to fortify the criminally inclined to commit antisocial acts.

It is true, especially in the past, that marijuana use was greater among groups who committed a higher-than-average number of petty crimes, but there is no indication of a cause-and-effect relationship. There has never been any objective evidence to support a direct relationship between marijuana use and major crime. In fact, the evidence is undeniable that, other factors being equal, alcohol is more closely associated with aggression and violence than is marijuana.

It must be emphasized that marijuana use definitely represents a real danger in terms of driving cars and piloting planes, and this relationship is treated in detail in another chapter of this book.

Is the use of marijuana beneficial?

Many discussions of marijuana concentrate exclusively on whether or not it is harmful, as though its use were an exercise in seeing how long one could hold one's hand in a fire without getting burned. Obviously, users feel they get rewards, or they wouldn't use it. Marijuana provides a rather reliable means of relaxation from tension and anxiety, and produces a mild change in consciousness, which its users find a pleasant diversion from the normal state of mind. Throughout history, the human race has always sought consciousness alterations, by chemicals and by a large variety of other methods. In the past, it abandoned itself to festivals or dances and achieved dramatic changes in consciousness. Historically, religious practices such as meditation, chanting, and other rituals also have produced these effects. Primitive humans discovered such methods as fasting and isolation to bring about these altered states. Young people today are probably much more aware of various ways of "turning on" and achieving altered states of consciousness through both drug and nondrug methods than were their parents.

The occasional use of drugs to attain such states is not inherently any worse or better than the use of nondrug methods. What makes drugs potentially more dangerous than many other methods of altering consciousness is that their use is easily repeatable and requires no active participation on the part of the user. This is an important difference, because methods that require the individual to participate actively are usually self-limiting. On the other hand, the drug route is passive and may be repeated at will. Young people are especially vulnerable in this respect, since they frequently lack the perspective and experience to exercise restraint over such non-limiting behavior.

In addition to the pleasure motivation for the use of

marijuana, it is sometimes claimed that its use increases creativity, or in other ways improves one's normal capability. Some of these claims have been objectively tested—especially in the area of musical performance. The results have been uniformly negative. It is possible that the loosening effect of marijuana can make for more spontaneity or emotionality in certain artistic performances, although its potential in this regard is limited. More often, what is encountered is the rationalization of heavy users that they function better while under the influence of marijuana. These claims are not borne out in fact. Such people are enthusiastic about the creative things that go on in their heads, but they seldom carry through to finished products. Excessive use of marijuana and the self-discipline necessary for creative productivity seldom go together.

A WORD ABOUT THE MARIJUANA LAWS

At one time, most of the federal and state laws controlling marijuana were essentially the same as those covering heroin and the other opiates. Almost all marijuana violations were defined as felony offenses and were punishable by prison sentences. Some of the violations required mandatory prison sentences of five to ten years or even longer, without possibility of parole. Recently, many of the penalties for marijuana offenses have been reduced, especially those directed at the user. Because most of the recent violators of the marijuana laws are young people who are not lawbreakers in other respects, many judges have been going around the existing laws to avoid imposing severe sentences. Eleven states have made the possession of small amounts of marijuana a civil offense punishable by a fine, but others still treat possession as a misdemeanor criminal offense, and a few still carry felony penalties. Large numbers of young people are involved in selling it to some degree, and every day hundreds pay heavy fines and go to jail. This is a hazardous activity, not only because of the risk of arrest, but because of the temptation to become involved in more lucrative large-scale marijuana dealing or other drug trafficking. Such escalation is likely to result in very serious criminal involvement.

The trend toward lesser penalties for marijuana use seems likely to continue, and it may be that most criminal sanctions at the user level will be removed within a few years. Some Western countries have already followed this policy. It appears unlikely, however, that marijuana will be given the same legal status as alcohol and tobacco in the near future. In the meantime, a person who chooses to use marijuana may be taking a considerable risk over and above any harm attributable to the drug itself.

SUMMARY

Marijuana has a history of thousands of years, and its use as an intoxicant is second only to that of alcohol. It belongs to the family of drugs known as hallucinogens, but its effects are much milder than the stronger drugs in this group, such as LSD, mescaline, and psilocybin. Hashish is a more concentrated form of the drug. Hashish is used in Eastern countries, but in this country its use is less prevalent than marijuana. Marijuana is generally smoked, although it may be taken by mouth as an ingredient in food or drink. It produces a mild alteration in consciousness consisting of a sense of well-being, relaxation, and euphoria. Senses are often subjectively heightened, although performance of most physical and mental tasks is impaired. With larger doses of marijuana, and especially when hashish is used, pronounced distortions of perception and thinking somewhat similar to those caused by LSD may be produced.

The physical effects of marijuana use are still controversial, and many young people are changing their attitude about marijuana. The evidence does seem to indicate that pregnant women should not use it. Marijuana will occasionally produce panic reactions, especially with large doses, inexperienced users, or when used in a threatening environment. On rare occasions these have developed into temporary psychotic reactions.

Marijuana is not physiologically addicting; however, a small proportion of users do become psychologically dependent on the drug, in the sense that it plays an integral part in their lives. In these cases, its use can contribute to a number of undesirable consequences. Heavy users often concentrate largely on their immediate needs and impulses, adopting an unrealistic attitude toward the future and toward their environment. As a result, they frequently ignore basic health requirements as well as economic responsibilities, fail to develop a discipline for self-expression, and adopt a pattern of naive magical thinking, as opposed to rationality and common sense.

Among the present population of users, marijuana rarely leads to the use of addictive drugs such as heroin. On the other hand, the use of marijuana does sometimes serve as an introduction to LSD, amphetamines, and other dangerous drugs. There is no evidence that marijuana use causes crime.

Overall, marijuana is the least harmful of the drugs currently being illegally used by young people (marijuana, cocaine, LSD, PCP, amphetamines, and barbiturates). *There are, however, very real dangers attached to its frequent use.*

It should be stressed that, as with alcohol, the initiation of significant use during adolescence involves considerably more risk of developing into disruptive or disorganized behavior than does adult initiation.

ALCOHOL ABUSE

Margaret O. Hyde

The number one drug abuse problem in the United States is alcoholism. Alcohol has been called the most dangerous drug of all. Even the people who do not agree with this statement agree that, with the exception of nicotine, there are more people addicted to this drug than any other. The estimated number of alcoholics ranges from 10 to 14 million, with from 6 to 10 million more who have drinking problems. About 3 million alcoholics in the United States are under the age of 18.

Alcohol is neither good nor bad, but what people do with it can make a great difference in their lives as well as the lives of others. As noted in the chapter, "Mind Drugs and Driving," the drunken driver is everyone's problem. About 56 million people, those who are members of the families of alcoholics, are directly affected. Many of these people are children who feel they are in some way responsible for a parent's drinking problem. Many of these children suffer from physical as well as emotional abuse.

The FBI reports that large numbers of crimes are committed by people who have been drinking heavily.

A recent report by the Bureau of Justice Statistics showed that more than half of convicted jail inmates admitted that they had been drinking enough to feel "pretty drunk" or "very drunk" just before committing violent crimes. The social costs of excessive use of alcohol are estimated to be billions of dollars annually. The cost of human suffering cannot be calculated. Fortunately, research in the development of a test that may spot alcohol problems in the early stages is creating a great deal of excitement.

Many of the old ideas about alcoholism are changing. For example, there are many images, such as the skid-row bum, the man who experiences "lost weekends," the person suffering from D.T.'s (delirium tremens), or just from severe tremors and fever as a result of too much alcohol. These are common illustrations, but most alcoholics do not fit any of these pictures. You may know one and not even recognize him or her as a problem drinker.

The problem drinker is no longer considered a big joke by intelligent people. At one time, stage drunks amused audiences, and real drunks were considered more sickening than sick. Today, people are looking deeper into the causes of alcoholism and seeing the problems there. Such problems are no joke. Those who abuse alcohol probably shorten their lives by ten to twelve years.

Many people do not recognize the fact that they are problem drinkers. Dr. Morris E. Chafetz, former director of The National Institute of Alcohol Abuse and Alcoholism, is an expert in alcohol problems. He suggests that a person needs help if he or she has any of the following experiences: goes to work intoxicated, drinks in order to work or get to work, drives a car while intoxicated, is injured bodily and requires medical attention as a result of being drunk, gets in trouble with the law as a result of drinking too much alcohol.

Why is it that about one in ten who drinks suffers from a drug abuse problem, in which the drug is alcohol? Why do they do it in spite of the fact that they hurt their bodies? Some answers to these questions are beginning to appear, but much remains to be learned. Since many people do not think of alcohol as a mind drug, alcohol *abuse* has suffered from a laissez-faire attitude. Today, new awareness of the extent of the problem of alcoholism is helping to initiate greater efforts in prevention, education, and research.

If one decides to drink, knowing how to drink responsibly is obviously of great importance. Knowing about alcohol abuse is important in gaining an understanding of drugs that affect the mind.

What is severe alcohol abuse, or alcoholism? The American Medical Association identifies alcoholics as "those excessive drinkers whose dependence on alcohol has attained such a degree that it shows a noticeable disturbance or interference in their bodily or mental health, their interpersonal relations, and their satisfactory social and economic functioning." Another definition comes from the National Council on Alcoholism. They describe an alcoholic as a "person who is powerless to stop drinking and whose drinking seriously alters his or her normal living pattern."

No matter what the definition, there is general agreement that alcohol can be addicting. With more and more drinking, the same amount may be tolerated to a greater degree, so that the drinker craves larger and larger amounts. When people drink to excess in spite of the consequences, they have become alcoholics. The craving for alcohol can exceed the will to live.

Perhaps you are asking, "What are my chances of becoming an alcoholic if I drink socially at any time in my life? Does heredity have anything to do with it? Is one woman's body chemically different from another's in such a way that she is prone to alcoholism? Is the problem purely one of emotional or psychological origin?" Certainly, there must be many causes, and the research to find out more about the causes of alcoholism is complex.

Scientists know what happens to the human body when a person drinks an alcoholic beverage. To a druggist or pharmacologist, alcohol is a drug that is classed with anesthetics such as ether, for its action is much the same. Once the alcohol is absorbed by the body through the lining of the stomach or small intestine, the first areas to be anesthetized are the parts of the brain that act as control centers for the higher mental processes. Inhibitions are lessened and the result is a spurt of activity in which people do things they would not do otherwise. This is often described as "getting high." Many people speak or sing in loud voices, or feel important and excited.

Normally, about 98 percent of the alcohol that one drinks is turned into heat or energy, but the warming sensation described above occurs long before the oxidation of alcohol in the body produces the heat or energy. Most scientists believe that a person can burn about one twenty-fourth of a fluid ounce of alcohol per hour for twenty-two pounds of his body weight. The time required for all the alcohol in one beer, or four ounces of table wine, to leave the body of a 160-pound person is two hours. If you sip an alcoholic beverage containing one ounce of pure alcohol over a period of one hour, your body will be burning up alcohol at about the same rate that you absorb it. It takes about six hours for four beers consumed in one hour to leave the body of a person weighing 160 pounds, and the effects on feelings and behavior, which also last six hours, include difficulty in performing motor skills and reduction in vision and hearing. A slight speech defect may be present. A six-pack of beer consumed in one hour produces uncoordinated behavior, definite impairment of judgment and memory, and decreased inhibitions, and it takes from six to eight hours for all the alcohol to leave the body. Heavy drinkers may show fewer symptoms, but impairment starts long before a person becomes drunk. Most people can judge if they are drunk because they can feel it, but they cannot judge impairment.

Usually unconsciousness prevents people from drinking themselves to death, but there have been cases in which so much was drunk so quickly that the brain centers controlling breathing and circulation were paralyzed before the anesthetic action produced unconsciousness, and death resulted.

Since getting help as soon as a problem develops is

stressed by many experts who work with the alcohol abusers, knowing how a person can tell if a drinking problem is developing is especially important. The following test is suggested for young people by Alcoholics Anonymous World Services:*

Answer Yes or No:
1. Do you miss days or class periods at school because of drinking?
2. Do you drink to overcome shyness or build up self-confidence?
3. Is drinking affecting your reputation at school or elsewhere?
4. Do you drink to escape from study or home worries?
5. Does it bother you if somebody says maybe you drink too much?
6. Do you have to take a drink to go out on a date?
7. Do you ever get into money troubles because of buying alcoholic beverages?
8. Have you lost any friends since you began drinking?
9. Are you going with a crowd of heavy drinkers?
10. Do your old friends drink less than you do?
11. Do you drink until the bottle is empty or the beer cans are all dead?
12. Have you ever had a loss of memory from drinking?

(* Used by permission of Alcoholics Anonymous World Services Inc., New York)

13. Have you ever been stopped by the police, arrested, or put into a hospital or jail because of drunk driving?
14. Do you get annoyed with classes or lectures on drinking?
15. Do *you* think you have a problem with drinking?

A "yes" to one question is a warning.

A "yes" to as few as three questions means that alcohol has almost certainly become—or is becoming—a serious problem.

The list of diseases associated with chronic alcoholism is long, including such serious illnesses as cancer of the liver and other vital organs, brain atrophy, damage to the pancreas and kidneys, impotence, premature aging, heart attack, and other cardiovascular diseases. Alcohol causes changes in the release or uptake of important chemicals that control communication within the brain. Continued abuse of alcohol leads to alcohol-related diseases that account for 30 to 50 percent of all hospital admissions.

How do people who become addicted to alcohol differ from those who drink socially and only occasionally? Causes of alcoholism vary with each case, but many people have definite opinions about the reasons for excessive drinking. Some religious groups consider alcoholism a sin and all drunkenness as the result of irresponsible behavior. Social scientists view alcoholism as a social dysfunction, stressing the influence of environment on the person. Most authorities recognize alcoholism as a disease and there is growing evidence to confirm that many alcoholics have a difference in their biological makeup that plays a part in alcoholism. Research has shown that alcoholics do not metabolize alcohol the way others do. A genetic reaction to alcohol is thought to play a major role in the development of alcoholism in about 50 percent of the cases. It has long been noted that alcoholism runs in families, and new research is throwing light on why this is true. Certainly the problem is complex.

For some teenagers, alcohol is a way to blot out a terrible aspect of their lives, such as poverty, physical or sexual abuse, or the loss of a parent through divorce or death. Many young people use alcohol as an escape from poor self-image and other emotial problems or as a form of rebellion against what they consider excessive parental controls. Teenagers who have a family history of alcoholism have an especially high risk of becoming alcoholics at an early age.

Although problem drinkers still constitute far too large a group of people, the movement toward greater concern about health has led to a significant decrease in the average consumption of alcohol by people of all ages. Americans are becoming more conscious of the health effects of drinking and increasingly antagonistic about those who drink to excess. Even liquor companies have joined in nationwide efforts to educate young adults about the danger of alcohol abuse.

Many young people feel more comfortable about saying no to offers of alcoholic beverages in this new climate in which there is great concern about healthy bodies. They accept the fact that drinking is no longer a necessary part of the sophisticated life-style. Who wants to jog after a night of heavy drinking?

In many schools, groups of students have banned together to work toward the prevention of drunken driving. As the number of nondrinkers has grown, the number of nonalcoholic parties, proms, discos, and other forms of entertainment have appeared on the scene. Organizations such as BACCHUS (Boost Alcohol Consciousness Concerning the Health of University Students) and Students Against Drunk Driving are acting to promote safe and responsible drinking on college campuses. Many colleges are calling for bans on alcoholic beverages at sporting events and offering counseling for students with alcohol problems. They are observing Alcohol Awareness Week and promoting nonalcohol bars. But alcohol abuse continues to be a problem on many campuses.

Although drinking is less important to many students than in the past, one out of every ten high school and junior high school students in a recent New York State questionnaire described themselves as "hooked" on alcohol. Some said that they had been drunk in class. One in ten got drunk at least once a week.

Many young members of Alcoholics Anonymous say they have a dual problem of alcohol and other drugs, and other studies show that younger alcoholics tend to abuse drugs in combinations. According to a report in the *Journal of the American Medical Association*, alcohol abuse in early adolescence is a strong predictor of later alcohol abuse and other drug problems. The number of children who begin drinking at an early age has increased in the last few years and those who begin drinking early tend to drink more. In a recent study of some sixth graders, the percentage who drank at least once a week doubled in a period of one year. The pattern of drinking has changed, too. Many children drink to get high rather than to relax or for help in socializing as their older brothers and sister did.

The journey from alcoholism to health may take many different paths, for it is a complex medical, emotional, and psychological problem. Psychotherapy, combined with the program of Alcoholics Anonymous, seems to be one of the most preferred treatment approaches. Certain drugs, such as antabuse, have been widely used to discourage alcoholics from drinking. If the patient takes such a drug and then drinks an alcoholic beverage, he or she becomes very ill, vomiting, sweating, flushing, and getting depressed. Many alcoholics abandon this treatment before they give up their craving for alcohol, a craving that can be greater than the will to live. Such deterrent drugs do not cure a patient's problem, but they may be helpful in bringing him to the state of seeking further help.

While Alcoholics Anonymous can be considered a form of group therapy, and about half those who join can make a healthy adjustment without the help of a psychiatrist, many do need special treatment. There is a growing closeness between Alcoholics Anonymous and psychiatry, and a growing mutual respect.

For some young people, the problem of alcohol is one that they must face because they have an alcoholic parent or relative. Some are members of groups such as

Alateen, an organization designed to help the young family members of alcoholics. There are over 2,000 groups throughout the United States and foreign countries, some as far away as Ghana. Any teenager can get information about the nearest group by writing to Alateen, Post Office Box 182, Madison Square Station, New York, New York 10010. Meetings consist of discussions where young people can exchange problems and get a better understanding of themselves and their confused home situations. It helps them to lose their shame about their relative as they learn to understand more about alcoholism.

Many children of alcoholics blame themselves for a parent's excessive drinking. New programs in schools and mental health clinics are trying to erase the "burden of guilt" which many of these children carry because of their anger toward parents. Programs aim to increase self-esteem, help children to cope with life in an alcoholic home, and rebuild the family unit. Many experts believe that alcoholism is a family-centered problem, regardless of whether the alcohol abuse is found among the parents or the children.

When a parent is a very heavy user of alcohol, a child stands greater than average chance of becoming a victim of child abuse, neglect, molestation, and incest. These young people, in turn, frequently veer toward antisocial behavior, neurotic symptoms, psychosomatic complaints, and are more likely than others to develop alcoholism themselves, according to Loran D. Archer, Acting Director of the National Institute of Alcohol Abuse and Alcoholism. Treatment programs for the children of alcoholics should be stressed and should be made available to anyone who wants help. Many children of alcoholics can be helped easily and dramatically in fairly short periods of time.

Certainly much more needs to be learned about the abuse of alcohol. New approaches that emphasize the search for causes, prevention, and early treatment are helping to shed light on this badly neglected problem—a situation in which some people anesthetize themselves to the point where they love alcohol more than life.

LSD

Duke D. Fisher, M.D.

Dr. Duke D. Fisher has had extensive experience with LSD users. He is a neuropsychiatrist and was Assistant Clinical Professor of Psychiatry at the University of California School of Medicine.

Although LSD use declined after the mid-1960s, this drug is still being used illegally. In recent years, alleged samples of LSD that have been analyzed in the United States and other countries usually did contain some LSD, although the amount in each sample varied from just detectable amounts to up to nearly 500 micrograms. Any amount over 120 micrograms is regarded as extremely dangerous. In fact, LSD has been called the most dangerous of drugs that are abused. LSD continues to be available on the streets of the United States and Europe for people who request it.

What is a "good trip" as compared to a "bad trip"? The good trip occurs if the LSD user has primarily pleasurable experiences. Some people say that they can "hear colors" and "see sounds." A trip is a highly personal experience and no two people experience it exactly alike. Some people see intense colors and have feelings that are foreign to them. Some individuals experience the feeling that their body is leaving them or that they are two people. Some people consider this drug experience to be completely unlike their previous life experiences. Some experiences they believe to be mystical or semireligious. A bad trip, or "bummer," occurs when a person becomes frightened or finds the LSD-induced experience to be so unpleasant that he or she seeks help. Many bad-trippers go to hospitals, emergency rooms, ministers, or friends to get help. During the past several years many young people have reported bad trips. Physicians call bad trips adverse reactions to LSD. There have been many articles in medical journals describing some of these adverse reactions.

We started seeing many young people coming to our hospital at UCLA because of bad trips. We studied the first seventy patients who came to our emergency room to find out what kind of symptoms they had with their bad trips. The most common symptoms we found were the same as those of people suffering from a persistent psychosis, those who live in an unreal world. Some people would take LSD and their trip would continue beyond the usual twelve to eighteen hours for LSD effects. Many individuals continued to hallucinate, continued to be paranoid—extremely suspicious with delusions of being watched, criticized, or persecuted. They were convinced that people were going to hurt them or that animals were chasing them, or they continued to be out of contact with reality. An example of this kind of reaction was a teen-age boy who locked himself in his room because he thought he was an orange and that if someone touched him, he would turn into orange juice. He was able to live because a few friends would bring in food for him; however, he remained locked in his room for several months. This type of false belief is called a delusion. We found delusions to be quite common among young people who had taken LSD. The second most common symptom was severe depression—many times with suicidal thoughts. We talked to many young people who were convinced that they had to die because they felt so unworthy. One young girl broke a Coke bottle and cut both of her wrists after she had taken LSD at a Hollywood nightclub. Some individuals are successful in their suicide attempts. The third most common symptom we saw in the emergency room was anxiety to the point of panic. Many people would become quite frightened at the fact that they were losing control of themselves under LSD. One college student had taken LSD and had an accident on the freeway. He was so anxious that he ran up and down the freeway until the police were able to restrain him and bring him to our hospital for treatment. The last, most commonly observed symptom was confusion or wandering about. Many LSD users were brought to our hospital not knowing where they were going or who they were. Some of these people would be found wandering around the beaches or the city at night. Many of them were malnourished and had physical difficulties because of long exposure to the sun.

How do we treat patients with bad trips? Some of the patients were so disorganized and psychotic that long-term hospitalization was necessary. Some of the patients who were very nervous and agitated had to be given large doses of tranquilizers. Some were able to return to their families or friends after a few hours; however, it was necessary for us to hospitalize and provide longer treatment for many of the LSD users. Some bad trips would last for months, and even large doses of tranquilizers and hospitalization would not help the patient. There have been some patients who did not respond to treatment and had to be sent to state hospitals for long-term care. One young girl who took LSD was on a bad trip for four months. We were finally able to stop her unpleasant experiences by giving her fifteen electroconvulsive treatments. These are treatments in which electrodes are attached to the scalp, and the patient is given electrically induced seizures.

It is difficult for police to enforce the law that prohibits possession of LSD. The drug is a colorless, odorless, tasteless substance, often applied to the back of an envelope or a postage stamp or put into clothing; by licking the postage stamp or the envelope or chewing on the clothing, one can have an "experience." LSD is supplied in sugar cubes, capsules, tablets, liquid, or practically any other form. The usual dose is between one hundred and two hundred micrograms. You can put enough LSD in an eye dropper to "turn on" or provide an LSD experience to 10,000 people.

The average dose of LSD is sold for five to ten dollars. We have had samples of black-market LSD analyzed and found that many times there are impurities present. LSD users do not know how much LSD they are purchasing, and we have found a wide range of doses that were many times much less, and, in a few instances, much greater than the dosage that was thought to be purchased.

There was a great deal of interest about LSD in terms

of its psychedelic, or "mind-expanding," properties in the 1960s. This interest led to a great deal of emphasis on psychedelic clothes, music, and art. Psychedelic clothes and art usually included intense colors. However, many people who participated in psychedelic art shows and psychedelic "happenings" did not use drugs.

LSD is erronenously called a mind-expanding drug, when really it is quite the opposite. The attention one can pay to the ordinary details of life is diminished after using LSD. The drug knocks out that part of the brain that has to do with filtering incoming questions. Consequently, a person who has taken LSD is aware of a multitude of stimulations, such as whispering, breathing, or people walking, that most of us filter out when we are paying conscious attention to some episode in our surroundings. A person on a trip is also aware of intense internal stimulations, such as the hallucinations previously mentioned, internal fantasies, or dreamlike experiences. These internal stimulations make it equally difficult to pay conscious attention to what is really happening in the outside world.

What are the physical effects of LSD? They are few. Dilated pupils is the most common effect. Sometimes people on an LSD trip wear sunglasses even at night to protect their dilated pupils from bright lights. There is also a transient chilliness, skin flushing, increase in blood pressure, increase in pulse rate, and increased respirations.

LSD is not physiologically addicting. This means that there are no withdrawal symptoms when one stops using it. The drug may be psychologically addicting, since a psychological need to keep using it may develop. There is no known lethal dose for humans, or known overdose. One tragic fatality occurred with an elephant in Oklahoma. Here researchers calculated the dose of LSD on the elephant's massive body weight instead of its tiny brain weight. The elephant received a massive overdose of LSD, convulsed, and died.

There are two special points concerning the "freak trip," or adverse LSD reaction. First of all, it is unpredictable who will have a bad experience. No psychiatric interviews, psychological testing, or stable life and job histories can screen out adverse reactors. I have seen people who are apparently normal have very severe reactions to LSD. Doctors, lawyers, other professionals, and people who seemed stable have become very disturbed after using LSD. Conversely, I have seen many people who are very disturbed and who had histories of severe emotional difficulties have no ill effects from using LSD. In other words, just because someone seems to have no emotional problems, he or she will not necessarily have a good trip.

It is possible to have recurrences of the original symptoms up to three years after taking LSD, without using the drug again. There are various conditions that can stimulate a recurrence of the original trip. When some people are angry, upset, feel intensely about a personal problem, listen to certain kinds of music, or look at intense lights, they will have a recurrence. One young girl always had her recurrences on the freeway. She would be driving at night and rather than seeing one pair of headlights, she would see a thousand pairs of headlights and not know which were real. One man became frightened that a girl friend would kill him during his original LSD trip. He no longer uses LSD. However, he has a paranoid recurrence, and many times he has had the idea that his girl friend is trying to hurt, or possibly kill him. He has been having these flashbacks, as they are sometimes called, for two years without using LSD again. Physicians use certain tranquilizers to reduce the anxiety and to diminish the frequency of these flashbacks experienced by some users. Some people report only a few flashbacks occurring every month; nevertheless there have been some patients who have reported having fifteen to a hundred flashbacks per day.

Are there side effects in the LSD users in the community who never seek aid? Yes, and this has been one of the most interesting parts of our investigation. My associate and I attended "acid-head" parties at Big Sur, California, and gatherings around the beaches, visited college students using LSD in Berkeley, California, and spent time in the Haight-Ashbury area in San Francisco. We found many LSD users who were disorganized, quite confused, and having flashbacks, but not seeking medical attention. We also found nonsuicidal deaths occurring after using LSD. Some deaths occur because the user experiences perceptual changes. One young girl leaped to a rocky beach thinking that the ocean had turned into a silk scarf. There were two young boys who felt they were having a religious experience and wanted to "become one" with several cars on Wilshire Boulevard. I had to restrain one young student who believed he had the new power to fly and attempted to leap from a window in a Hollywood apartment. There are undoubtedly more accidental deaths never recorded or attributed directly to LSD.

What about set and setting? Set is one's attitude toward the LSD experience, and setting is the physical environment in which one takes LSD. Set and setting are important but not 100 percent important. There is a great deal of mythology about LSD, including the idea that if you feel relaxed, take LSD with a friendly guide or a sitter, and have soft lighting, you won't have a bad trip. This is untrue: we have had many patients in our hospital who had all of these things going for them but still had bad trips.

What are the long-term changes in one's attitude, personality, and motivation after using LSD? Unlike many drugs, LSD does not require chronic use for one to have these changes. We have seen some individuals manifest long-term changes after using LSD only once or twice. Many young people, after using LSD, have a dramatic change in their value systems. We have talked to high-school students and college students who dropped out of school after using the drug. Professionals, business people, and artists become much less interested in their former pursuits and more interested in mysticism, withdrawal, and preoccupation with the effects of LSD. When Timothy Leary said, "Turn on, tune in, drop out," he was describing an observable social phenomenon. We met a gentleman at a Hollywood Hills party who had spent months wandering around the desert near San Bernardino contemplating his LSD experience. Prior to using LSD he had been an international lawyer in New York City. Another long-term change is a feeling of improvement but an objective loss of functioning. We have spoken with many people who felt they were more creative, that they had greater problem-solving ability, and that everything seemed less complicated after using LSD. Nevertheless, when we studied their lives closely we found they seemed to be doing much worse. We spoke with a mathematical engineer who maintained that after taking LSD he could do problems that normally required three to four hours in ten to fifteen minutes. Further questioning determined that he had lost his job. His reply to this fact was, "No one understands my answers anymore—but that's their problem." The perceptual distortions caused by LSD result in users having the feeling that they are doing better, while in reality doing much worse. LSD can give people the idea they are much stronger or have more powers than normal people. We spoke with one group who claimed to have extrasensory perception after using LSD. They felt they could read minds and "pick up vibrations" from other people. Our studies revealed that they did no better reading minds than if they would have merely guessed; however, they had the feeling that they were doing better.

Some people develop a missionary quality after using LSD. They are no longer content to take the drug themselves, but have the feeling that they should "turn on" everyone. We recently hospitalized a young mother who was giving her eighteen-month-old daughter LSD. One man became so enraptured with LSD that he took his life savings and purchased all the LSD he could, and marched up and down the beaches near Santa Monica passing out LSD to everyone he met—until he met a narcotics officer.

Another long-term effect of LSD seems to be that LSD users have difficulty tolerating feelings that occur in close relationships. "Love-ins" and "love sessions" were gatherings that we frequented for several months. We found that many young people, while talking about love, had a great deal of trouble communicating with others. This is reasonable, since LSD leaves the user with greater self-preoccupation and with less psychic energy available really to care about another person. We found many LSD users describing their "love for humanity," "love for the world," and "love for nature"; however, they had a great deal of difficulty loving one other person.

Why are so many young people attracted to LSD and hallucinogenic drugs? Most of them are quite curious and concerned about who they are, what they are, and what is important in life. Many young people can be convinced the answer is to be found in a capsule, a tablet, or a sugar cube. LSD and the hallucinogenic drugs distort one's abilities to find real solutions to important problems. Young people are extremely concerned about their feelings. This is the time in life when a young person is dating, gets involved in all types of activities, and is very interested in society and the way it should be changed. Some young people with personality problems attempt to avoid their sexual and aggressive feelings by using LSD. The substance creates a drugged state or psychedelic effect that gives users the illusion that they have solved some of their problems with feelings, when actually they have merely pushed them out of the way for a period of time. It is normal for young people to find different ways of accommodating their feelings, such as dating, political action, writing, or self-analysis. In a sense, LSD robs them of a chance to find solutions by creating the illusion that there are no more struggles. We talked to one who said: "I don't have to hate anyone anymore, as long as I continue to use LSD and drugs." A young girl told us: "I am not interested in boys anymore and sex has no meaning after using LSD." The drug actually diminishes one's sexual and aggressive experiences.

Are abnormal babies born to mothers who have used LSD? Many people have been very concerned about what LSD can do in terms of birth defects. There have been about two hundred research projects dealing with the potential of LSD for producing birth defects and chromosomal changes. The overwhelming majority of these yielded negative or highly questionable results. Nevertheless, medical researchers believe that it is most unwise for pregnant women to experiment with *any* drugs and especially those of questionable nature.

Should you turn on with LSD if you are in good health, not pregnant, and looking for a mind-altering experience? Why not turn on, tune in, and drop out? There are no easy answers for these questions. Young people must make this decision for themselves. It is difficult being a young person today. Society is far from perfect. Young people realize they have had adult heroes who so often were models of drug abuse. It is sometimes difficult not to use drugs when one's friends maintain that this is the only way to "be in." Young people are curious, and most of us know that if someone really wants drugs they are available. Nevertheless, it is important to receive the facts about LSD and other drugs. It is difficult to tell someone else what to do with his or her brain. I believe that if young people receive information about drugs, they are in a good position to make their own decisions. However, some people, because of serious psychological problems, are driven to using drugs as a defense against life and their feelings. But the majority of young people do have a choice. In a way, taking LSD is like playing Russian roulette. Some people use it with very few unpleasant experiences and seem delighted with the intense colors, the hallucinations, or the distortions that occur. Nevertheless, for some, LSD is a psychotic nightmare, and can mean several years in a state hospital, flashbacks, and long-lasting personality changes.

It is unfortunate that there exists such a generation gap in our society today. Many adults discount anything that young people say. Similarly, some young people dismiss anyone over thirty as being "an old fogy" or "out of it." It is important to build bridges between these two generations. It is obvious that the Establishment does not have all the answers. One has only to take a look at the alcoholism, the suicide rate, and the social problems of today to realize that the Establishment needs help from young people who are willing to consider new ideas. There are those who would say: "Forget the whole thing and drop out." I can't agree with this philosophy. Teenagers can use their energies and ideas to change society. "It is better to light just one small candle than to curse the darkness."

HEROIN

Margaret O. Hyde

"Where can I go for help?" is a frequent question these days. It comes from a heroin addict in a small town in the Midwestern part of the United States. It comes from a young boy in Harlem, where heroin is available at the candy store. It comes from very young people and from very old.

Today there are many places where help is available, although not nearly enough. The kind of help is not always the same. Perhaps this is a good thing, for each individual differs. There are as many heroin problems as there are people addicted to it. The answer for some people lies in one kind of rehabilitation, while others seek a different kind of help. For many, the question has only a negative answer. There is no place to go. There is not enough money. There is not enough knowledge.

There is nothing but to wait and hope.

Karen is an accidental heroin addict. She was in the wrong place at the wrong time. She admired Charles and his friends and thought that heroin use was one of the "games people play." She knew it was dangerous, but she admired the daring of Charles and the other users. The danger seemed romantic and attractive, and she drifted into trying the drug so that she could feel less alone, one of the group. Today Karen knows that with heroin there are no winners and she is one of the addicts who are asking, "Where can I go for help?"

Karen is not very different from many of the others— the boy in the city, the girl at the ski resort, or any of thousands of others who have found themselves in similar trouble. Karen may well be the junkie next door.

Ralph came home from Vietnam after using heroin for a short time. He had picked up the habit when men in his company were trying to escape the boredom and the hassle of life in Vietnam. Drugs helped him to forget. He had smoked marijuana, and at one point couldn't get any from his friends. Someone told him that everyone was going with scag (heroin), so he tried it and found it was a great experience. It was easier to hide from the authorities, because there was no odor; and friends assured him that he would not become hooked as long as he smoked it and did not inject it into his veins. So he packed heroin inside his regular cigarettes and smoked away. Actually, no matter how you take it, heroin has a high potential for addiction, but Ralph's experience was very limited.

When Ralph returned to the United States he was able to stop his use of heroin after a period of rehabilitation. He returned to an entirely different life-style from the one he had known in combat and to a place where the drug was not easily available. He continued to remain drug-free for a period of time. This was not the case with some of his friends who had been using drugs before they entered the service and who returned to a life style in which heroin use was common.

For many people in the United States a supply of narcotic drugs is a need that must be met if they are to feel normal. Some of these people have become addicted after long experiences in hospitals where drugs have been prescribed to help them cope with pain. Some have become addicted through experimentation with illegal drugs. The kind of person who is a heroin addict does not always fit the picture that so many people have, any more than the "skid-row bum" fits the description of most alcoholics.

Actually, there have been many eminent people who suffered from narcotic addiction, including doctors, lawyers, and a congressman. These people lived normal lives since they were able, through various means, to supply their needs and maintain a stable level of the drug. One of the most interesting cases is that of Dr. William Steward Halstead, who became dependent on cocaine through experimenting to find a new method of anesthesia. He conquered the hold of cocaine by turning to morphine and continued this dependence for most, and perhaps all, of his life. The secret story of his involvement with drugs was kept in a "black box with silver key" and opened after his death at age seventy. During his life he was a brilliant surgeon and one of the four founders of the famous Johns Hopkins Hospital in Baltimore, Maryland. He was also an addict who was able to control his craving by daily administration of an exact dose of morphine.

No one knows how many people are addicted to heroin. There are an estimated 400,000 to 750,000 heroin addicts in the United States spread from city ghettos to college campuses and prosperous suburbs. Although there was a decline in the number of young adults using heroin after the 1970s, recent reports show that new use is occurring among people who use cocaine intravenously. Users report a plentiful supply of heroin.

Heroin is sold only through the black market, and supplies continue to reach the United States in spite of strenuous efforts to control the flow. When the smuggling of heroin from Southeast Asia via the laboratories of Marsaille (the French Connection) was curtailed, the supply from Mexico increased. Heroin continues to come from countries such as Burma, Laos, and Thailand (The Golden Triangle) and Pakistan, Afghanistan, and Iran (The Golden Crescent). An unusually potent new form of heroin called black tar is coming from Mexico. In recent years, black tar has made Mexico the largest exporter of heroin to the United States.

In addition to the usual problems that go with heroin addiction, two new dangers have been added. The heroin bought may turn out to be unusually potent and lethal designer drugs produced in laboratories by underground chemists. They are called designer drugs because they are designed with molecular structures slightly different from illegal narcotics. Designer drugs, that are copies of amphetamines and hallucinogens, have been available since the 1970s, but recently drugs that are more difficult to copy have appeared. Copies of heroin and other narcotics are just slightly different from the drugs that they imitate. Often, the synthetic drugs are more powerful. At least 20 people died from overdoses of one synthetic drug that turned out to be 1,000 times more potent than expected. A slightly different version of a drug that can produce effects like heroin was responsible for a number of tragedies. Two addicts who injected themselves with this drug literally "froze" with needles stuck in their arms because the drug destroyed cells in their brains that control movement. Some users developed a disease similar to Parkinson's disease. There are versions of synthetic drugs that are so potent an amount that would fit on the head of a pin could kill 50 people.

Another recent danger for heroin addicts was added when AIDS (Acquired Immune Deficiency Syndrome) appeared in the United States in 1981. AIDS is spread by sexual contact and by the transfer of blood. Intravenous drug users share needles, and if they use needles contaminated by the AIDS virus, they can become infected. AIDS is a life-threatening disease that damages the body's ability to fight invading bacteria, viruses, and other infections.

One approach to the prevention of the spread of AIDS is to educate heroin addicts about the risk of sharing needles. About 15 percent of the people with AIDS fall into the category of intravenous drug abusers. Children born to mothers with AIDS become infected before birth, during birth, or from breast feeding. Drug abusers who are warned to protect themselves from the disease by pamphlets distributed by various health organizations are told that the best prevention is to stop injecting drugs. However, the physical addiction makes it difficult for them to heed such advice.

Dealing with the addict's physical dependence on heroin is only the tip of the iceberg. An addict may go through withdrawal or detoxification and be free from physical addiction in weeks or months, but the craving can still remain. Without professional help, an addict may once again begin the cycle where very little matters but the next "fix," the injection of heroin into the vein, which makes all problems seem to vanish. When the effect wears off, he is back on the narcotics treadmill. He is once more in a race against time, where he spends all his energy securing heroin for the next round in the vicious cycle. The addict is really the prisoner of the cells of his own body. Now his body needs the drug in order to function properly. He lives in a world of petty thievery, cheating, treachery, and dirty, unkempt rooms, alternating with hospital and prison stays. Getting the heroin powder, cooking it with water in a bent spoon to make it a liquid, injecting the preparation into his vein with a needle inserted into an eyedropper; these activities makes his world. *No one who has not lived in this world knows the power of its hold.* This is the heroin story. This is a story for which there was no hope, for which there was no solution in the past.

Fortunately, many people have come to realize that addicts are sick and their criminal acts of stealing, etc., are a part of a vicious cycle that enables them to avoid withdrawal. Today there are ways of coping with the addiction problem that are better for both the addict and society. When addicts are considered sick, they can be treated as patients. But helping addicts is still experimental, and can be as demanding of patience as the curing of cancer.

In the effort to cure, many search for the roots of addiction. Certainly, this is a complex matter, for each person has an individual heredity and environment.

Each person is different from every other one. Many general suggestions of motives have been made, such as escape from problems that are much too great for a person to handle: boredom, decay of family life, poverty conditions, fear of the future, loneliness, anxiety, despair, curiosity, peer pressure, as well as physical predisposition.

Many heroin addicts have low-grade emotional problems or character disorders before they become addicts. Even if they do not, their life develops into one in which they lie, cheat, and steal in order to get the drugs that they need. One patient describes his experience in the following words:

> Nobody knows *why* he goes on drugs. Everybody can tell you *how*. "They" say it's because of the environment, being from a poverty-stricken area, or being brought up in a broken home, or things like that. But there are people with the same problems who don't take drugs, and there are people from good homes, wealthy homes, not broken homes, and they do take drugs. Maybe it's all in the head, as "they" say, but I don't remember having any psychological drive to take drugs. It's just that you're going with the crowd, and they're all taking drugs and you want to be "in" and so you try it.

Although in the past detoxification and psychotherapy succeeded on a very small number of patients who were under constant medical care, it did little to help the huge numbers who suffer from heroin addiction.

The search for a chemical to blockade the narcotic

effects of heroin began at Rockefeller University under the direction of Dr. Marie Nyswander, with a very small group of patients who had long histories of drug abuse. They had tried psychotherapy without success. When they were maintained on morphine, there was no antisocial drug-seeking behavior, but the patients were not able to return to society and carry on normal living. They sat in front of the television set, watching passively. They waited for their next shot of morphine, and their interest ebbed and flowed with the rhythm of these injections. When the drug methadone was tried, the change was striking. The patients lost the gray look that is typical of addicts, they took greater interest in their personal appearance, and began talking of their future plans. One patient taught himself to type. Arrangements were made to continue with education and plan for the future. One patient worked through three years of high-school curriculum in eighteen months, with A grades, and continued at an engineering college where he enjoyed a normal and active social life.

The drug methadone, under proper medical supervision, frees the addict of drug hunger without producing euphoria, and without the need for an increase in doage. Under proper medical supervision, a single daily dose achieves the blockade of the narcotic effect. Today, this methadone-treatment program is being supplemented by educational, vocational, and supportive services such as psychotherapy and group therapy as fast as treatment can be made available. Clinics have sprung up from St. Thomas to Montreal, from New York to California. The methadone-treatment program has spread to almost every state in the United States and throughout the world. Some clinics provide methadone only during the withdrawal period; others include methadone maintenance and counseling.

Studies have shown that maintenance of a drug-dependent woman on methadone under close supervision can raise the likelihood of a safe pregnancy and the birth of a healthy infant whose own withdrawal symptoms are readily controllable.

The success of the maintenance program, as described in the next few pages, depends a great deal upon *proper* medical supervision and guidance. Since methadone itself is addictive, it must be administered by a licensed medical doctor or nurse. Misuse can cause death. But when it is properly prescribed, it acts as a normalizer, or stabilizer, rather than a narcotic.

Suppose you are a heroin addict who wants to become free of the swing from brief euphoria to sickness. You are tired of a life that depends on getting large sums of money, dodging the police, and being interested only in searching for and using drugs. You want a new life that does not revolve around the driving need to secure enough narcotics to get through each day. You have been accepted at a local methadone center.

You begin with the first step in treatment, a process known as stabilization. This involves finding the smallest dose that will fit your individual case. Your tolerance depends on the size of your previous habit, and you are given amounts that will help you to reach a maintenance level so that you will no longer crave heroin, and you will no longer be a sick human being as you were before. Any medical problems that you have in addition to the heroin addiction can be treated at this point. After Phase I you become an outpatient who reports to the clinic for a daily dose of methadone for at least a year. During this length of time (Phase II), you will get help in continuing your education or finding employment.

Methadone maintenance permits the helping professionals to work with the wider problems involved in heroin addiction. While methadone is not a cure, it does make patients accessible to help by bringing them back regularly to a clinic for needed services or for referrals to community facilities. For many people, some kind of maintenance is needed for normal functioning for long periods of time. According to Dr. Vincent Dole of Rockefeller University, it is unrealistic to expect a limited period of maintenance to produce a high rate of abstinence in people who have been addicted for a long period of time. This is especially true if narcotic drugs leave an imprint on the nervous system and the drug-seeking behavior that follows has a neurochemical cause. Still, this is a subject of controversy. The discovery of natural opiates within the body adds a new dimension for a possible biological basis for addiction.

The time of discharge from a methadone-maintenance program should be based on individual situations, but many treatment clinics have been forced to discharge patients to make room for the admission of new ones, due to lack of funds. As new patients enter methadone programs, the majority of persons who have left treatment relapse, creating a revolving-door situation.

The cost to society is much less for those in treatment than the social costs of relapse, which include crime to supply money for drugs and possible maintenance in prison if the criminals are caught and punished. It is difficult to understand why our society tries to cut costs by discharging patients and discouraging re-entry into programs.

A number of experimental drugs are being tested in clinical treatment programs for heroin addicts. One, naltrexone, was approved for use by the Food and Drug Administration on November 28, 1984. Naltrexone had been tested on at least 2,000 addicts over a period of many years with a high rate of success among highly motivated middle-class addicts, such as physicians and other health professionals, but the rate of success for "street addicts" was described as low.

Naltrexone is an antagonist. When it reaches the surface of certain brain cells, they act something like a wrong key that gets into a lock but won't turn. This wrong key prevents other keys from getting in, and in this case prevents the action of drugs such as morphine and heroin, making them pleasureless.

Some drug treatment experts are concerned about the use of naltrexone on addicts with liver damage, a problem which many addicts have. Dr. Herbert D. Kleber, Professor of Psychiatry at Yale University School of Medicine, and others who have studied the problem for many years believe that a substantial number of addicts can take naltrexone without adverse effects.

The nondrug approach to helping heroin addicts has been used for many years with varying degrees of success. These programs, known as therapeutic communities, emphasize changes in personality and life-style with emphasis on freedom from all drugs that affect the mind. Therapeutic communities, such as Daytop Village and Phoenix House provide a structured environment where staff and addicts work together to change behavior. They believe that people are not fragile, but that they can be confronted with their condition and challenged to grow into maturity and responsibility.

Life at a therapeutic community usually includes encounters, or "attack therapy," in which the here-and-now feelings of an individual are examined by a group of people. Conversations may become verbally violent and openly hostile. Thirty-hour group therapy marathons, seminars, public-speaking opportunities, community relations, and lectures all help in the attempt to have individuals understand their personality structure and to live without chemical crutches or physical violence. Since employment is viewed as a major treatment goal by the therapeutic communities, as well as by other types of programs, there are efforts toward preparing residents for jobs.

How effective are different kinds of treatment? No one knows the answer. No one really knows why some people are more susceptible to addiction than others. But what is known is that there is a need for more research and for more treatment programs. Young people who are exposed to mind drugs, parents, taxpayers, and all citizens in every walk of life should be concerned with the complex problem of heroin addiction.

DRUGS AND DRUG DEPENDENCY: WHO AND WHY

J. Martin Myers, M.D. and
Kenneth E. Appel, M.D., Ph.D.

Dr. J. Martin Myers, Emeritus Psychiatrist-in-Chief of The Institute of Pennsylvania Hospital, and Dr. Kenneth E. Appel, a former President of the American Psychiatric Association, are authors of this chapter.

There is a great deal of difference in potency and effect among mind drugs. There is a great deal of difference in the social acceptance of the use of these substances and their effects. There is a terrible and dangerous difference between the effect of the caffeine in a cup of tea or coffee and that of a drug like "speed," or Methedrine.

Perhaps the question is not the peril of a drug-oriented society so much as what kind and how much of a drug should be accepted. Another important aspect of the problem is who uses drugs. Addiction studies in which rats administer morphine to themselves show that these rats become addicted, but when the animals receive the drug passively they do not. This suggests that a hospital patient who receives a drug passively is less likely to become addicted than a doctor who gives himself an injection for his own pain or fatigue. The "why" seems to have some effect, too.

The reasons that a teenager or young adult may use drugs that alter the mental or emotional state are many. There are no simple answers to why an adolescent uses drugs. The reasons may have nothing, or very little, to do with the pharmocological or physiological or medical action of the drugs, or they might be highly specific for the drug's effect on the user's feelings and personality.

Adolescence is a period of great psychological turmoil. Endocrinological changes and bodily developments heighten awareness of sexual drives. Each teenager must resolve questions of sexual behavior through an adjustment between family and social mores and his or her own conscience. Establishment of moral and ethical values, choice of vocation, selection of life partners, as well as learning the meaning of mature love—all these confront adolescents. They need to differentiate themselves from their parents. In doing so, they usually go through certain self-assertive outbursts of greater or less duration and intensity, which are often referred to by adults as rebellion. As they experience this important and essentially healthy questioning and casting off of some of their parents' values, they need the support of a group with whom they belong and of which they feel a part. It is for this reason that fads are most common in this age group: teenagers test old values with the great support of the peer group.

Progress is indeed made by this kind of questioning. Some of the strictest conformity can be demanded by members of groups of nonconformists. The result of this is that adolescents fear not belonging to their peer group, and in seeking to grow up with their own individuality, they do not dare to be so individual as to differ from their friends. In this sense, one of the reasons a teenager may take a drug is that others are doing it; not to do the same is to be "out." At this stage in personality development, and in consideration of this "why," it is irrelevant that the group-accepted behavior involves a drug; it might as well have been a particular style of dress, hairdo, or slang expression. The motivations of the leaders of the group or gang who have been using the drug can be any of a number to be discussed later, but the group can be carried along with them. There can be truth in the statement of parents that their daughter "got in with a bad gang." The same need to conform that made her a good child because she followed her parents' standards can be transferred to those who take the place of parents and have different values and aims. This can lead to behavior characterized by the parent as bad. Many times, members of upper-middle-class suburban society, of fairly well-to-do, intellectually better-than-average families, do not recognize that they are as conformity-driven as any group in this country. To be like others, to have similar experiences, is a highly motivating factor in the behavior of both adolescents and adults.

Not every young person who tries drugs just to go along with the crowd becomes involved in drug abuse.

Just as a hospitalized patient is less likely to become addicted than a person who actively uses the drug himself, so a well-adjusted teenager is less likely than one with problems to use the drug to the point of psychological dependence.

Self-assertiveness and rebelliousness can be a large factor in motivating the teenager's actions and behavior. This rebelliousness is largely focused on the parents, the adult world, and the established values they stand for. As a result, teenagers at this stage of development might come to value certain things and behavior simply because the parent or social system disapproves of them. Again, the rationality or irrationality of the adult's disapproval is not in and of itself taken into consideration. There is satisfaction and a genuine value for adolescents who dare to confront previously established value systems if they do so within limits. They need to experience such negativism, but it is always a risk that this negative assertiveness may endanger themselves or others. They are constantly faced with decisions, both conscious and unconscious, of how much, how far, and what kind of behavior they can attempt. Drugs can be used for such expression just because they are disapproved of.

Another "why" depends on the social customs that have grown up around the use of some of the drugs. In the adolescent and young adult, the use of marijuana is generally carried out in groups, in the so-called pot parties.

The group gathers and proceeds with the preparations in an almost ritualistic manner. They "manicure" the seeds and stems from a batch of pot by shaking the mixture through a strainer. They roll the fine material into cigarette papers and fill a variety of pipes. Here is a special comradeship, a secret society, that each finds missing in the impersonal atmosphere of a large campus. Even the passing of the pipe can be felt as a shared experience and offers acceptance to the smokers. There are giggles, a rush of talk, a solemn ritualistic silence. This can be one of the most important parts of a student's social life on or off the campus, particularly for those who tend to have some feelings of estrangement from others.

Some are motivated by the fact that the drug is a drug, but not to the specific pharmacological action it produces. They want to experience something new, something different. Like the mountain that must be climbed because it is there, the drugs offer new excitement, new thrills. Those who have felt bored may particularly respond to stimulation that a drug might offer.

As the use of many mind drugs is forbidden by law, there may be some tension attendant upon breaking the rules and the uncertainty of being found out. There are those who like to try the risky or dangerous, who want to assert their bravado by fast driving or taking the dangerous drug. In addition to the tension increase and its release when the risk has been taken and managed, a user might have the added satisfaction of being admired for having taken a risk.

The reasons given above as to why the drug is taken are probably more important for the teenagers who take mind drugs on rare occasions, or who have tried them just once or twice. Usually the pharmocological action of drugs is more important for the person who is motivated to use the drug frequently, either alone or with other drugs. The most frequently sought-after feeling is the relief of anxiety, the lifting of the weight of depression and the simple escape from the pressures and tensions of school and community as well as the larger world.

Alcohol, of course, has been the most universally used tranquilizer for centuries. As a depressant of the higher center of the central nervous system, it allays the anxiety and uneasiness of millions. The worried student uses it for the same reason as the worried adult: it makes him feel better. For those who drink to try to lift their depression, alcohol carries a certain risk, for one of its aftereffects is to increase the depression. The social customs that have grown up around drinking offer approval of people using alcohol in a group to relax and become less socially inhibited.

The use of sedatives, such as the barbiturates (phenobarbital, Nembutal, Amytal, Seconal), and other hypnotics, such as Doriden, has been common. This group of drugs, plus other tranquilizers less productive of sleep, are used because they depress the central nervous system's sensitivity to external stimuli. They relieve feelings of tension and anxiety, and they dull the senses more than alcohol does, even though both may release some inhibitions, and heavy users may become violent. They are used excessively by people who have unbearable feelings of tension and anxiety and by stimulant abusers. When so used, the amount taken grows, and drug dependency can develop. Cessation of their use can cause jitteriness and in some cases convulsions.

Drugs such as Benzedrine (the pep pills) are taken for their stimulating effect. It can be physiological or psychological, or both. Some students first take them to stay awake in order to cram for exams. Some overweight individuals take them to curb the appetite. The third (and much more dangerous) reason is to do away with feelings of chronic fatigue or the "blues." The feeling of tiredness and lassitude may rapidly disappear and be replaced by an increase in pulse rate, blood pressure, and general alertness. The frustrated, unhappy person may enjoy this pleasurable state and seek to repeat such an exciting feeling. Although initially very small amounts do increase physical and intellectual alertness and do provide a sense of well-being for many people, tolerance rapidly develops. Larger and larger amounts need to be taken. Then, too, with the alertness and sought-for excitement there is frequently a very uncomfortable feeling of apprehension. The heart throbs and the person is jittery or even gets the shakes, so then he might take one of the sedative depressants. Or the stimulant's effect of wakefulness is more prolonged than desired, and the person can't get to sleep, so he takes a sedative. Such mixtures of a stimulant and a depressant to pick one's spirits up and combat the attendant jitters is known to be very risky as larger and larger amounts are taken. True drug tolerance and dependence are easily established.

Large amounts of stimulants such as Benzedrine and Dexedrine can produce very unusual behavior, such as tremendous fear, disorientation, and hallucinations. Small amounts of Methedrine, or "speed," can rapidly produce a psychosislike state accompanied by bizarre hallucinations. One strange thing that can happen during the use of speed is what is called being "hung-up." A person who is hung-up may get stuck in the repetition of an act or thought for hours. She may open and close a box again and again; she may sit in the bathtub all day; or she may clean the house over and over again.

A "speed freak's" hallucinations may differ from those of an alcoholic in that he may understand that the voices and strange ideas that come to him are caused by the drug and do not really exist. This type of paranoia may progressively disappear over the course of several months to a year if the drug is completely avoided. It rarely becomes permanent. But stimulants of this group (the amphetamines) have a marked effect on the heart and the circulatory system. Putting these under such a severe strain is particularly risky.

Marijuana acts differently from the depressants, alcohol, and sedatives, for its effect can offer more for the worried and troubled person who feels frustrated. It offers more than just the dulling of the senses to the hurts of living because it produces in some a feeling of well-being, a sense of euphoria. It increases the user's self-confidence and decreases her self-criticism. There is no question that such feelings are desirable; everybody seeks them. We may attain such self-confidence from successes in living. The less a person experiences a sense of well-being and satisfaction with her achievements toward desired goals, the more she might seek a drug-induced feeling as a substitute. The girl or boy who is self-conscious or uneasy socially may feel somewhat relieved after a drink, or with a mild sedative. Those who smoke marijuana may experience not only relief of the discomfort, but a positive pleasurable feeling. The person who has smoked "pot" is much less inhibited socially and feels confident in being able to discuss intellectual or other topics she wouldn't have dared to open her mouth about before. The dissatisfaction with grades that, even if high, are not as high as desired, is forgotten after dragging on "the weed." Her drive to be doing more and more in a compulsive fashion is relieved, and she can relax. Sexual inhibitions are decreased, so that greater sexual freedom is permitted within the group. The pleasurable aspects of the marijuana experience can be a powerful attraction for its re-experience.

Some seek the sense of great physical and mental ability that accompanies the state caused by marijuana. The user may feel unusually aware of her body. For instance, one user described states of near ecstasy on feeling her arms and legs move.

Perhaps in evaluating society's goals you find them too materialistic, and today's way of life too impersonal. All this may be more keenly felt in college. As the psychedelic or hallucinogenic drugs can produce a markedly heightened sensory experience, even illusions and hallucinations, many young people seek this specific drug effect with the purpose of counteracting so much of our mechanized, impersonal life. But does it really solve the problems?

Certainly there are times when you will feel uncertain about yourself, inadequate, not sure. Many decisions have to be made: how to use your time, how much to study, how to choose and make friends who are worthwhile, how to get along with the other sex, how to handle sexual impulses, how to accept necessary authority and, more important, how to think for yourself, weighing and judging the opinions of classmates and the adults whom you like.

Some young people make these decisions and adjustments with relative ease. They fill their time with activities that bring satisfaction, and when problems arise they work through them without too much stress. Others face great difficulties. Some feel overwhelmed with problems, and may find escape in drugs. Temporarily they may be relieved and feel their personalities enlarged, but these feelings do not last. There are dangers of wasted lives and great suffering. And the problem that started them on drugs is still unsolved. Obviously, there are other ways of feeling good, of learning to get satisfaction through achievement and success.

Society is changing, and it desperately needs to change. It needs the clearheaded thinking of young people who will share and take part in sustaining, organizing, and remolding our world. One develops individuality and identity, initiative and confidence, and self-decision by living, playing, and working in cooperation with others.

There is danger of getting sidetracked from the real problems and from the solid satisfactions of life. The irresponsible use of drugs is for the most part weakening and destructive, both to the individual and to society. Drugs are sidetracks not leading to fulfillment and genuine identity, individuality, and satisfaction. In fact, they cancel out these possibilities. Drug abuse may lead into hallucination, alienation, ineffectiveness, and disease. Ultimately it may lead to isolation and withdrawal, to unwholesome destructive dependency, to uncontrolled dissatisfaction and hostility, to violence and crime.

Those who withdraw and do not participate in building society have missed the joy that comes from the cultivation of self-resources, the exhilaration that comes from achievement. They miss the enjoyment of effective work, the satisfactions from recreation, play, and the arts. These satisfactions make reliance on drugs unnecessary and help people get away from them if they have temporarily succumbed. Enjoyment of work, collaboration with others, sustaining friendships with peers and/or colleagues, love, growth, self-development—all these are elements of satisfying living that sustain people in disaster, disease, and aging.

DRUGS AND DRIVING

Margaret O. Hyde

If today is an average day, 74 people in the United States will lose their lives because of drunk drivers. According to the National Institute of Justice, about 1,800 more will be seriously injured on an average day. Each person represents an incalculable loss. Many families are destroyed, and large numbers of victims are maimed for life.

Drunk driving is the leading cause of death and injury among those under 25 years of age. According to the National Traffic Safety Administration, drivers between the ages of 16 and 24 account for only 20 percent of all licensed drivers, and for less than 20 percent of total vehicle miles traveled, but they are involved in 42 percent of all fatal alcohol-related crashes.

Drugs other than alcohol are involved in at least 4 percent of all traffic crashes according to the Highway Users Federation of Safety and Mobility, and this estimate is believed to be conservative.

If you know just one person who has been the victim

of a person whose driving is impaired by alcohol or some other drug, you are probably one of the many people who are working toward the reform of laws to deter such accidents. Many Americans are calling for the mandatory jailing of drunk drivers, at least after the second offense.

Organizations such as Mothers Against Drunk Driving (MADD) and Students Against Driving Drunk and Students Against Drunk Driving (SADD) have exerted a great deal of pressure and this has resulted in some change. Since 1981, more than 30 states have enacted legislation directed at drunk driving control, most often by prescribing more severe sanctions such as mandatory confinement.

According to Remove Intoxicated Drivers (RID), the most important factor in controlling drunk driving is the activity of citizens at the local level. RID began in 1978 after Doris Aiken of Syracuse, New York, and some friends began researching what happens to the drunk driver in our criminal justice system. They wanted to know why drivers, even after killing or maiming someone, kept their licenses or received special permits to drive. Through the combined voices of victims and concerned volunteers, RID grew to over 155 chapters in 32 states and affiliates in France that have had an impact on laws and on the attitudes of the public.

Mothers Against Drunk Driving emerged shortly aftere RID through the tireless work of Candy Lightner whose 13-year-old daughter was killed by a man who had a long record of arrests for intoxication. MADD has well over 300 chapters nationwide and over 600,000 volunteers and donors. The group provides speakers for schools and community events, lobbies legislators for tougher drunk driving laws, and works toward new goals such as mandatory incarceration for repeat offenders. They point out that an estimated 30 percent of the drunk drivers arrested each year have been previously arrested on charges that were alcohol-related.

Teenagers have banded together throughout the United States and in many parts of the world in a movement to do something about the problem of drunk driving. Many groups, known as SADD, sprang up after the death of a young person in their community. Some groups call themselves Students Against Driving Drunk and others are named Students Against Drunk Driving, but no matter what the name, they are working toward removing the drunken driver from the road. Students Against Driving Drunk stress peer pressure and alcohol education. Since its founding in 1981 under the direction of a teacher who lost two students to drunk driving, as many as 8,000 chapters have been opened in high schools. The teacher, Robert Anastas of Marlboro, Massachusetts, has traveled extensively to aid in the formation of groups. The number of requests for information from SADD headquarters is large, resulting in a backlog of requests.

One of the most famous approaches to the drunken driving problem is SADD's Contract for Life. This is a contract between parent and teenager in which teenagers agree to call for advice and/or transportation at any hour, from any place, if there is a situation where they have had too much to drink or the person with whom they are driving has had too much to drink. The parent agrees to come and get the teenager, or pay for a taxi, with no argument at any time. The situation is to be discussed at a later date. The parent also agrees to seek safe transportation if he or she is in a similar situation.

Copies of SADD's Contract for Life can be reproduced from the appendix of this book or can be obtained by writing to SADD, P.O. Box 800, Marlboro, MA 01752. Many projects have been developed by this group to help students remove drunk drivers from the road.

The groups known as Students Against Drunk Driving tend to work toward forcing the government to take effective steps to get drunk drivers off the road as well as encouraging young people not to drink and drive.

Hopefully SADD-type organizations will be established in every high school. A handbook that will help anyone interested in forming such an organization is *Driving the Drunk Driver Off the Road* by Sandy Golden, Acropolis Books, Ltd., Washington, D.C.

A designated driver program is another approach to making the highways safer. However, there is a possible side-effect to this, since drinkers who know they do not have to drive may take this as a license to get drunk. Dr. Morris E. Chafetz, a famous authority on the subject of drinking and driving, suggests that a broad program to educate the public on how to control drunkenness would be far more effective than a designated driver approach. He notes that it has already been shown that many people have learned to preserve their health by giving up smoking, exercising more, changing their diets, etc. People should be encouraged to feel responsible for friends who overdose on alcohol, making them dangerous to themselves and others.

Public opinion is playing a part in enforcing laws that hold tavern and restaurant owners responsible for traffic accidents that are caused by people to whom they have served liquor. Court rulings have also held hosts liable for traffic accidents caused by guests.

Many myths about drinking continue to be held as fact by people of all ages. Here are some statements that are commonly believed. Some may be true in certain circumstances, but not always.

Myth Number One: "I'm O.K. to drive. I had plenty of mix in my drinks."

Although soda, quinine water, fruit juices, and other mixes dilute alcohol, the alcohol continues to be absorbed into the bloodstream. Mixes reduce alcohol's irritant effect on the lining of the stomach in some cases and may delay the onset and intensity of alcohol's effect; however, carbonated beverages may even decrease the time it takes for alcohol to reach the bloodstream.

Myth Number Two: "I can drive home safely. I ate a big dinner right after cocktails."

Although food slows the passage of alcohol into the bloodstream and dilutes the concentration of the alcohol, a person who consumes enough alcohol can be intoxicated even after eating a large meal.

Myth Number Three: "I know I'm not drunk. Even

my speech is quite clear. The alcohol in my system will not interfere with my driving ability."

Unfortunately, the degree of intoxication may not be obvious to a person or even to his or her friends. Many people are unaware that they have had too much to drink for safe driving. In a recent experiment, a radio announcer drank alcoholic beverages and gave estimates of his own condition to listeners periodically. While he considered himself still sober, it was obvious to others that he was not in any condition to drive home. Monitors of the experiment made certain that he did not drive.

Many volunteers are surprised when traffic researchers have given them just one or two drinks and tested them. These people did not feel any effect, but there was laboratory proof that they did not handle the steering wheel and brakes as well as they thought they could. That small difference in ability can be very important in an emergency. More than two-thirds of legally drunk drivers who were surveyed in a Canadian study thought they could drive as well as when they were sober.

Myth Number Four: "I'm an experienced drinker. I can hold my liquor."

Tolerance has been called the acquired capacity of not appearing to be as drunk as one really is. This does not mean that reaction time improves with drinking experience. A heavy drinker will not show the same effects in feeling and behavior as the average drinker. He or she often can have a high blood alcohol concentration

(BAC) with few observable effects, but judgment, vision, concentration, comprehension, and reaction time are all impaired.

Obvious drunken drivers are not so much a traffic problem as problem drinkers. It is estimated that there are about two million real problem drinkers on the road today, and many of them get home safely. But even though many of these heavy drinkers have learned to tolerate large amounts of alcohol, scientific tests show that no one can drink without impairing reflexes to some degree.

Myth Number Five: "A large person can drink all night and still drive safely."

While it is true that a small person becomes more intoxicated than a large one on the same amount of alcohol, large people can certainly become too drunk to drive safely. Body size does make a difference, but fat does not count.

Myth Number Six: "I can drink until it's time to drive home because I've been perspiring a great deal and that gets rid of the alcohol. Besides, I'll take a cold shower just before we leave."

Neither perspiring nor taking a cold shower is a way to sober up faster. Allowing time is the only way to reduce significantly the amount of alcohol in the bloodstream. Although a small amount of alcohol leaves the body through perspiration, it is almost impossible to "sweat oneself sober."

How much can a person drink and still drive safely?

There is no one answer to this question, since many factors are involved. Most people, under normal conditions, can drive safely if they have had one or two drinks over a period of several hours, but this is not always true even for the same person.

Since alcohol that is consumed faster than it is eliminated affects one's judgment, coordination, visual perception, and sense of balance, it is easy to see how this can impair driving ability. Deciding when a person is a menace behind the wheel of a car is more difficult.

Legal limits for driving are measured in terms of blood alcohol concentration (BAC) or blood alcohol level (BAL), a measure of the amount of alcohol in the blood. Suppose a man who weighs 150 pounds drinks five ounces of 86 proof whiskey in one hour on an empty stomach. Only a teaspoonful of alcohol reaches the one and a half gallons of blood he has in his body, making the alcohol content one-tenth of 1 percent (.10 percent). The legal limit in the United States is set by state law and varies from .08 percent to .15 percent.

Another way to understand BAC is to consider that .10 percent means that there is a drop of alcohol for every 1000 drops of blood in the body. Although this does not seem like much, this small amount of alcohol can change an excellent driver into a highway menace. He or she is six or seven times more likely to have an accident with a BAC of .10 percent than if no alcohol were present. If blood alcohol concentration reaches .15 percent, the chances of an accident are twenty-five times greater.

BAC can be measured directly by taking a sample of a

person's blood or urine and analyzing it, or it can be measured indirectly by analyzing a sample of a person's breath. In this method a person blows into a box, a portable breath tester about the size of a transistor radio, which is supplied by the police. Although breath testing is the most convenient, results from this kind of pre-arrest testing are not always accepted in courts of law. In many states, refusal to take a breath test is considered evidence of intoxication.

Laws vary from state to state about how much alcohol makes one legally drunk, but no legal definition is a real test of whether or not a person has been drinking too much to drive safely. Tests with professional drivers indicate that blood alcohol levels as low as .03 percent (one and a half beers for a 160-pound person) can have adverse effects on driving ability, decision-making, and judgment. Any amount of drinking impairs driving performance.

Much the same is true of other drugs. While the number of accidents caused by drunken drivers has been the subject of many studies, similar data about other drugs and driving are not available. A conservative estimate of 4 percent of traffic crashes caused by drugs other than alcohol translates into as many as 2,000 fatalities and 80,000 serious injuries each year. The actual figures are believed to be much higher.

In a recent study conducted by the Insurance Institute for Highway Safety, marijuana or cocaine was found, in addition to alcohol, in the blood of many male drivers killed in motor vehicle crashes. There is mounting evidence that cocaine and alcohol together are a lethal combination on the highway. Alcohol was found in 70 percent of such drivers, marijuana was found in 37 percent, and cocaine was found in 11 percent.

A combination of two drugs is believed to be more than doubly dangerous for those who are driving. A common problem among drug users is the belief that they are able to drive as well as without drugs. Even small doses of some drugs lull drivers into a false sense of confidence that makes them believe they are in control of a situation when they are not.

Limited surveys indicate that from 60 to 80 percent of marijuana users sometimes drive while high. Evidence shows that marijuana use at typical social levels definitely interferes with driving ability. For example, experimental subjects who have smoked marijuana showed impaired ability in laboratory tests on driving-related skills, on test courses, in simulators, and in actual driving performance. Tests show that such drivers are more likely to miss important visual clues, that they have narrower fields of vision, and that they tend to be slightly less coordinated. They have more difficulty staying in line (tracking), and they do not respond as quickly to sound. While some studies show that the use of marijuana tends to decrease risk-taking and that experienced users tend to show less impairment in driving skills than inexperienced users, typical social doses do impair driving skills. Any marijuana smoker's biggest driving problems ocur when he or she is faced with unexpected events.

Although mild tranquilizers may improve the driving skills of some anxious people, they have a slight effect in slowing reaction time even at commonly prescribed doses. Some also interfere with eye-hand coordination and affect the speed at which the brain processes sensory information, and many doctors neglect to warn patients about the effect of prescribed drugs on driving ability. Certain sleeping medications affect driving skills the morning after they have been used. Certainly, sleepy or overmedicated drivers are not good drivers. Cold preparations may contain drugs, such as antihistamine, that produce drowsiness. Reading the label on over-the-counter drugs may help to prevent accidents.

Stimulants, such as amphetamines ("speed"), and caffeine, make people feel more alert and do improve driving skills for a *limited* period of time. However, after people have taken stimulants, they tend to overestimate their performance and take more risks. Perhaps this is why actual driving records show that people who take amphetamines are slightly more accident-prone as they continue to take them. Heavy users are able to stay awake for long periods of time, but one accident study found that they were four times more likely to be involved in a crash than nonusers. This was attributed to the fact that these drugs make people less coordinated and more tense.

Although research on cocaine use and driving is limited, studies indicate that this mind drug can produce lapses in attention and concentration. This alone makes it a dangerous drug to be used in combination with driving.

While the caffeine in coffee may help a driver stay awake, it does not help to make him or her sober after drinking alcoholic beverages. A drinker may feel more alert after several cups of coffee and attempt to drive, but he or she is actually just as handicapped in many of the complex tasks involved in operating a car as before.

Alcohol, marijuana, and other drugs create problems for train engineers and pilots, too. Alcohol has been cited as a probable cause in about 8 percent of all private plane crashes. In a study reported in the November, 1985, issue of the *American Journal of Psychiatry*, pilots were tested on the relationship between marijuana and safe flying. Pilots were tested on a flight simulator after one, four, and 24 hours after each had smoked a cigarette containing 19 milligrams of THC, the equivalent of two strong marijuana cigarettes. They used the simulator to take off, climb to 700 feet, make two turns, and then descend and land. They had trouble landing on the simulated landing strip even 24 hours after smoking, coming twice the average distance from the center of the runway. One of the pilots even landed off the runway.

Laws that prohibit a pilot from flying while under the influence of alcohol are more difficult to enforce in the case of private planes than on scheduled airlines. While drinking is seldom the lone cause of an airplane crash, the effects of even a single bottle of beer or one ounce of whiskey immediately before a flight can cause "a significant impairment in airmanship" according to the Federal Aviation Agency. This is probably based on the fact that the effects of even a small amount of alcohol combined with fatigue can lower decision-making ability or reduce the skill that is needed to prevent an accident.

Although the proportion of fatally injured drivers found to be intoxicated has been decreasing in recent years, the problem still looms large. Between 7:00 P.M. and 3:00 A.M. on weekends, in some parts of the country, one driver in ten is legally impaired, or drunk. During the period between midnight and 4:00 A.M. on any night of the week, between 75 percent and 90 percent of all fatally injured drivers had been drinking prior to the crash.

More than half of all Americans will be involved in an alcohol-related traffic accident in their lifetime. You can help to change this.

NOW THE GOOD PART BEGINS: Alternatives to Drug Abuse

Allan Y. Cohen, Ph.D.

Dr. Cohen is Executive Director, Pacific Institute for Research and Evaluation, Adjunct Professor, John F. Kennedy University, and a clinical psychologist in private practice. He is a former drug user who stopped all illegal use of drugs after becoming disillusioned with their promise.

"Why would you want to use drugs?" asked the psychologist. His client looked him straight in the eye and asked back, "Why not?"

A lot of time and money has been spent trying to find out why people use drugs. Reading some of the articles in this book, you begin to get the idea that there are all kinds of causes for drug abuse—social and economic problems, personality difficulties, family hassles, boredom, curiosity, escape, excitement, pressure from peers, and many, many more. We realize that people have been raised in different environments. They have different needs and different motives, and they may grow up with different attitudes about taking chemical substances—whether cigarettes, alcohol, prescription medicine, or illegal drugs.

BACKGROUNDS

Americans use an incredible amount of legal and illegal drugs. Adults seem to prefer abusing the legal variety—alcohol, tranquilizers, nicotine in tobacco, or stimulants (like diet pills). Somehow people seem to have lost respect for the natural efficiency of their own bodies and minds. When they feel sick or mentally worried, the first thing they think of is "medicine." Billions of doses of dangerous mind drugs are prescribed by doctors, sometimes because the doctors don't know how to handle normal psychological problems, sometimes because the patients demand some kind of medication. Most researchers estimate that more than half the American adult population has a serious problem with the abuse of mind drugs.

Social scientists have almost given up some of their pet theories about the "weird" drug user. It now seems clear that we are in the midst of a drug-using society, a civilization that considers drug use natural and looks to external aids for the solution of internal problems. The use of mind drugs is a *style*, a style reinforced by adult behavior, by pharmaceutical company media advertising, and by the idea that all medical problems should be cured by drugs.

Drug users range from those who are just curious experimenters to those who are completely hooked. Most of the publicity in the early 1970s centered on heroin addiction, on the narcotic-dependent "junkie" often involved in crime to support the demanding habit. But heroin use is merely the tip of an iceberg. Other mind drugs might not be as dramatically addicting, but their effects can be dangerous, partly because they can also be subtle. New findings on the effects of THC (their principal active chemical) suggest that "grass" and "hash" may have accumulative negative effects on the nervous system and especially on the personality and mind. Heavy users, who smoke more than once a week, may have some cumulative effects. Since these effects occur gradually, they never suspect that the cause is marijuana or hashish.

ALTERNATIVES TO DRUGS

People continue to take drugs even when they are aware of unhealthful side effects. The classic case is cigarette smoking—the "mature" adults in our society have shown a remarkable resistance to giving up cigarettes, knowing the health hazards involved.

This type of behavior helps us to understand a "mystery" about drug abuse that may point the way to some solutions. The secret is an observation often overlooked because it is merely common sense: *people use drugs because they want to.* They get some enjoyment from drugs, even if the enjoyment is temporary. People use drugs in the hope of feeling better, whatever that might mean for each individual. Unfortunately, most drugs seem to exact a more precious price than the "high" they give, the fun they provide, or the relief they temporarily produce.

Psychologists and educators say to drug users, "You know that drugs are bad for you, physically and mentally! You've seen the damage that drugs have done to friends of yours! But you keep doing it. How can we convince you to stop?" The young person takes it all in and quietly challenges, "Show me something better!"

This tells us a lot about preventing drug abuse before it destroys a person's chance to make a life for him- or herself. People *will stop* using drugs as soon as they find *something better.* People are not as likely to *start* serious drug abuse if they have *something better going for them.* The "something better" is what we might call an *alternative to drugs.* The common denominator of all successful drug abuse prevention and treatment programs is their ability to provide the potential users, the experimenter, or the addict with meaningful and satisfying alternatives.

When we talk about "alternatives" to drugs, we do not mean the same thing as "substitutes" for drugs. One crutch is not necessarily better than another. A young heroin addict might give up "junk" in order to join a violent street gang; this might be a substitute, but it is not a very constructive alternative. Another thing to realize about alternatives is that no one alternative is relevant for everyone. There is a pertinent saying in the drug field: "Different strokes for different folks." We know that people abuse drugs for different motives and needs. Sometimes these motives and needs come from *deficiency,* from serious problems. But other times there are *positive* needs causing drug experimentation, like the desire for adventure, curiosity, or the urge to explore oneself. Since people have varying needs and aspirations, the alternatives replacing drugs must also vary.

Generally, alternatives must be stronger as drug dependency gets stronger. The hard-core heroin addict has to be faced with a very involving alternative. Many successful former addicts have undergone deep spiritual conversions. Others have been rehabilitated through a tightly controlled residential therapeutic community where they could neither obtain drugs nor kid anybody about who they were.

When children first start out in school, it is possible to provide them with much subtler alternatives—like a real joy for learning, respect for themselves and their bodies, and the ability to understand and enjoy other children. The more people have good feelings about themselves, the better they can appreciate and relate to others; the more they know what is important in their lives, the less attraction the drug experience will have for them. It is not so much that drug-free people are afraid of drugs—educators have not been successful in *scaring* students out of drug use—it is more that they have better things to do than getting "stoned" with chemicals.

When some teachers and students decided to get together to do a drug survey at a high school near San Francisco, a questionnaire was devised and circulated by students; replies were anonymous. At that time, about half the students were using drugs. In addition to other questions, the *nonusers* (about 400) were asked the question, "If you do *not* use drugs, what has been the biggest deterrent for not using them?" The 260 completed responses to this open-ended question were categorized and gave the results shown in Table I (page 142).

From this table we find a very interesting trend—the greatest percentage of reasons given reflect *positive* reasons for not using drugs; only a few mentioned fear of

TABLE I. REASONS FOR NOT USING DRUGS

BIGGEST DETERRENT FOR NOT USING DRUGS	PERCENTAGE OF STUDENTS*
1. No need (i.e., life is fine; I'm happy or I turn on other ways)	39.8
2. Concern about interfering with physical and mental health and athletics	22.4
3. Because of the laws (i.e., respect for the law or fear of getting busted)	7.1
4. Brains and good judgment (i.e., having them)	6.2
5. Fear of the unknown	6.0
6. Seen results in other people	4.9
7. Out of love and respect for parents	4.4
8. Fear of addiction	3.4
9. Friends (i.e., peer pressure against drug use)	3.2
10. Other (not yet been contacted to take drugs, personal values or religion, unfavorable past experience, poor quality of drugs, don't know, etc.)	10.2

* Percentage adds up to over 100 percent because of some multiple answers.

something bad happening. It turns out that natural alternatives compete very well against drugs. If they are given a chance they are usually found much preferable to the temporary and artificial chemical experience.

TYPES OF ALTERNATIVES TO DRUGS

There is one primary step in promoting this new approach to the drug problem—getting people to think about alternatives and to apply the principle to themselves. A parallel trend we see is a new appreciation of the natural environment. The beauty and desirability of unspoiled air, water, and open space is increasingly a matter of concern. Ever since the 1960s, Americans have become more and more alert to the necessity for avoiding and reducing pollution. The same consciousness has been turning to the purity of foods and the undesirability of artificial and perhaps dangerous ingredients. Today, more and more people are becoming aware of "health pollution" and are trying to be moderate in drug use as well as avoiding other toxic chemicals.

Before mentioning other types of alternatives, it might be good to mention one alternative rarely discussed—the discontinuance of drug use. Many moderate drug users find that they feel much better (physically and mentally) after they stop their drug use. Even long-term users of marijuana report rather dramatic improvements (according to their own judgments) three to twelve weeks after they stop using mind drugs.

Of course, the structure of our social institutions has much to do with whether or not many kinds of alternatives are available to the general public. Part of the more general cause of the drug-use explosion has been the inability of government and society to meet adequately individuals' legitimate aspirations. These same deficiencies in society make the application of viable alternatives very difficult and slow. A good example of this is our elementary and secondary school systems. With some real exceptions, school is likely to be an uninspiring and sometimes meaningless experience for many students. In many places, the school curriculum is built around the world of students of twenty years ago. Most schools still stress competition and the importance of grades; this interferes with the joy of learning. Much of the material covered in the classroom has little application to the practical problems encountered by students. Many old-time teachers are very reluctant to explore the area of students' *feelings*; and yet, the emotional and mental state of students is critically important to them when decisions about drug use have to be made.

In a true "alternative school" situation, teachers are allowed to innovate and get "turned on" by the subject, thereby transferring this enthusiasm to students. Since teachers are possible models, they would, ideally, be relatively free from drug dependency and be able to communicate the feeling of the "natural high." Students would be given feedback, but not graded—especially in so-called extracurricular areas like art, music, physical education, manual arts, homemaking, drama, etc. After all, students should be able to develop real interests in leisure or career activities, freed from the debilitating pressure and anxiety that comes from worrying about how good one is at a particular subject. If a person finds something valuable in his or her life, whether it is a hobby, a talent, a purpose, other people, etc., the lure of drugs loses its luster.

EXAMPLES OF NATURAL ALTERNATIVES

In order to be more specific, let us look at examples of natural alternatives. One way of categorizing alternatives involves *areas of experience*. These areas of experience—from physical to spiritual—correspond to the kinds of gratification people seek when they use drugs. There is a lack in some area of experience and people try to use drugs to fill that deficiency.

One level is the *physical*. Here the person may use drugs to try to improve his or her sense of physical well-being. Examples of alternatives (there are scores more for each level of experience) might include the following: dance and movement training; physical recreation, e.g., athletics, exercise, hiking, and nature exploration (for *fun*); relaxation exercises, physical (*hatha*) yoga, and proper training in the martial arts, e.g., aikido, karate, judo.

Some people use drugs to gain satisfaction in the *sensory* area—involving the desire to enhance or stimulate sight, hearing, touch, or taste. Examples of alternatives include such things as: training in sensory awareness (balance, coordination, small-muscle control, etc.); visual exploration of nature; and the learning and practice of responsible sexuality.

One of the areas most commonly stressed in the study of drug abuse is the *emotional* level of experience. Here people might turn to drugs to gain relief from psychological pain, in an attempt to solve personal problems, or to eliminate anxiety or gain some measure of emotional relaxation. Natural alternatives in this area might include: getting a trusted professional to give counseling or psychotherapy; educational instruction in the psychology of personal development; and emotional awareness exercises, e.g., learning "body language," self-awareness, and psychological awareness.

A key area of alternatives is the *interpersonal*. It is no

secret that many use drugs to try to gain acceptance and status from friends and peers or to break through interpersonal barriers of one kind or another. Natural alternatives include a whole host of possibilities, some being: getting into a group of friends who are not serious drug users; experiencing well-run group therapy or counseling sessions; family life education and training; emotional tutoring, e.g., big brothers and sisters helping younger people; and creation of community "rap centers."

A rarer type of gratification sought by drug users involves the *mental* or *intellectual* level. They try to escape mental boredom, gain new understanding in the world of ideas, to study better or satisfy intellectual curiosity. Drug-induced insight is rarely enlightening—the author knows of a respected scientist who made an incredible "discovery" under LSD; for weeks afterward he walked the streets telling everyone he saw that "two plus two equals four!" There are more natural possibilities, e.g., intellectual excitement through reading, discussion, creative games and puzzles; training in hypnosis under qualified teachers; creativity training; and memory training.

In the 1960s there was quite a bit of talk about the *creative* or *aesthetic* level of experience related to drugs. People tried to enhance their experience or productivity in the arts. (Some people still cannot stand to go to a concert unless they are high.) Yet natural alternatives work out better for the artist or appreciator of art and music. Alternatives might include: nongraded instruction in the performing or appreciation of music; creative hobbies, e.g., crafts, sewing, cooking, gardening, and photography; and experience in communications skills such as writing, public speaking, conversation, etc.

Another subtle level might be called *stylistic*. Here the user is caught up in certain styles, e.g., the need to identify through imitation of adults or the desire for achieving things instantly. Alternatives can include: exposure to others who are meaningfully involved in non-chemical alternatives; parents agreeing to cut down on their own drug use; and exposure to the philosophy of the natural, appreciating the great possibilities of inner human resources.

An area often overlooked but with great potential for dissatisfied drug experimenters is the *social*, including the notion of *service to others*. Some may be desperate about our social and political situation and try to forget it or rebel against it through the fog of drugs. The alternatives are not only more constructive, but can be very fulfilling on a personal level. In the political area, people can be involved and work for particular candidates or in nonpartisan political projects, as in lobbying for environmental groups. One of the most powerful sets of alternatives, available to almost everyone, consists of getting involved in social service—helping others. This could include: helping the poor; providing companionship to the lonely; helping those in trouble with drugs or family problems; or helping out in voluntary organizations (like YMCA and YWCA, Girl Scouts, Boys' Clubs, Big Brothers and Sisters, etc.).

Another experiential level, the *spiritual* or *mystical*, attracted many users of psychedelics. Psychologists and sociologists are beginning to discover that they underestimated the power of the drive for spirituality. Some people hoped that drugs would give them direct spiritual experience, going beyond the limits of orthodox religion; they hoped to get a vision of God. For these people drugs can be very seductive because certain chemicals can induce illusory religious experiences that seem very real to the user. Even though a user may be temporarily inspired, too often she chases after this mirage and cannot apply what she thought were profound mystical insights. In contrast, growing in popularity are nonchemical methods for spirtual understanding and experience. These include such approaches as: study of spiritual literature; meditation and yoga; contemplation and prayer; spiritual song and dance; and increased exposure to different techniques of applied spirituality. In the spiritual area as well as the other areas not every alternative offered is of the highest quality. As we become more sophisticated about alternative means of inner growth, we shall become better able to discriminate the really helpful approaches from the hollow or misleading ones.

The examples given above do not cover every level of experience; indeed, some readers might like to categorize alternatives in very different ways. There are some examples that we might call *miscellaneous*. These relate to other needs such as the need for risk-taking and danger, the desire for adventure or exploration, the need for economic success, and combinations of various other motives. Here one might think of alternatives such as: sky diving, scuba diving, and "Outward Bound" survival training; vocational counseling leading to meaningful employment; and the possibility of gaining school credits for actual work experience in the community.

HINTS FOR THE ALTERNATIVES SEEKER

The use of mind drugs demands that people be *passive* and *uninvolved.* The lure of chemical intervention is that you can get something for nothing—by swallowing, smoking, or injecting you get happiness at a low price. But the evidence shows the contrary. When someone possesses the drug style, it possesses him back. But it is not always fair to criticize the drug user. After all, he is merely falling for the cultural line; he is going along with the prevailing philosophy that deep down, people are not really worth that much and have to be enhanced by some outside agent.

But times are changing. A few years ago, in many circles, it was more hip to use drugs; now it is beginning to be more hip to go beyond drugs. But how does one choose the way of going beyond? For some, it is no big problem—drugs are not that attractive; life is involving and meaningful, if not always easy. Other searchers may not be getting much help from their families, schools, or communities—they may not recognize the need to assist in the provision of alternatives.

The individual searcher must be alert. If she wants to be happier and more fulfilled, she must *try.* A great alternative in itself is the *process of putting energy into finding alternatives.* There are other guidelines that may be helpful. Be optimistic. If you have used drugs, ask yourself what you enjoyed about the drug experi-

ence; ask what areas in your life need work and fulfillment. Then *seek*, particularly in the areas of your highest interest. That means asking about different
alternatives you hear about or read about. Follow up
leads, investigate possibilities. One useful way is to discover the secrets of those you really admire—whether
friends, peers, or heroes—in order to find out what turns
them on. It can help to ask anyone who might know
about interesting avenues of exploration, especially former drug users. Look for help and ask for help if you
need it. Stay off drugs as much as possible while looking;
it will help you to evaluate the alternatives. Get others
to join you in the search. Have faith in yourself and the
possibilities of natural alternatives.

The problem of drug abuse is both a tragedy and a
challenge. It raises issues that every responsible human
being should face. The search for viable alternatives can
be, at the same time, great fun and very profound.
When honestly faced, the challenge of self-discovery
can force new perspectives on the game of life. In the
words of the great spiritual master Meher Baba, "To
penetrate into the essence of all being and significance
and to release the fragrance of that inner attainment for
the guidance and benefit of others, by expressing, in the
world of forms, truth, love, purity and beauty—this is
the sole game which has intrinsic and absolute worth."[1]

[1] Meher Baba, "The Place of Occultism in Spiritual Life: III,"
Discourses (San Francisco: Sufism Reoriented, Inc., 1967) Vol. II,
p. 110.

STREET
LANGUAGE

Street language varies from place to place. Some terms have several meanings and not all may be indicated here.

"A" .... amphetamines, speed.
ACAPULCO GOLD . a supposedly superior grade of marijuana, somewhat gold in color and supposedly grown in the vicinity of Acapulco, Mexico.
ACID .... LSD
ACID HEAD .... an LSD user.
ACID ROCK .... a type of rock music using electronic sound which is associated with the use of hallucinogens.
AMT.............. amphetamines
AMYS .... amyl nitrate
ANGEL DUST ..... phencylidine (PCP), a synthetic drug or animal tranquilizer. When abused, PCP has a higher percentage of undesirable effects than any other hallucinogen.
ARTILLERY .... apparatus used for the injection of a drug.

BAD .... drugs that are considered very potent or very good.
BAD TRIP .... a frightening reaction after the use of a

hallucinogenic drug, which can cause a temporary or chronic psychosis.

BAG .... marijuana; a small square of paper folded into a rectangle in order to hold a powdered drug; small plastic coin collector's bag used to hold powdered drugs

BAG .... a measurement of heroin or marijuana

BALE .... a pound of marijuana

BARBS .... barbiturates

BEANS .... benzedrine

BEAT .... counterfeit drug

BENNIES .... benzedrine in tablet form

BENT .... being a state of drug euphoria

BENZ .... benzedrine

BERNICE .... cocaine ?

BHANG .... the Indian word for marijuana

BIG C .... cocaine

BIG MAN .... the person who supplies a pusher with drugs

BLACK MOTE ..... marijuana that has been cured in sugar or honey, then buried for a period of time

BLACK HEROIN ... Mexican heroin that has the consistency of black tar and is more potent than conventional powdered white heroin

BLOW YOUR MIND to lose touch with reality and not have mental control

BLUE AND RED ... secobarbital

BLUE BULLETS.... amytal sodium

BLUE DOLLS...... amytal sodium

BLUE HEAVEN .... amytal sodium or morphine

BLUE MIST .... LSD

BLUES .... sodium pentathol

BOGART .... keeping marijuana to oneself

BOMBER........... a large-size marijuana cigarette

BOMBITA	cocaine and amphetamines in solution
BONITA	lactose crystals (milk sugar) often used to cut, or dilute, a drug
BOUNCING .... POWDER	cocaine
BROCCOLI	<u>marijuana</u>
BUSH	marijuana
C	cocaine
CACTUS	peyote, mescaline
CAN	about one ounce of marijuana
CANADIAN BLACK	marijuana grown in Canada
CANADIAN BLUES .	methaquolane
CANDY	drugs
CANNED SATIVA ..	hashish
CARGA	Spanish for heroin
CARTWHEELS	amphetamines
CAT	heroin
CHALK	amphetamine tablets that crumble easily
CHARLES	cocaine
CHARLIE	one dollar
CHICHARRA	Puerto Rican slang for a mixture of tobacco and marijuana
CHICAGO GREEN .	dark green marijuana
CHICK	heroin
CHINESE RED	brown heroin from Mexico
CHINESE WHITE ..	heroin that is pure white and very potent
COCA PASTE	made in the process of extracting cocaine from leaves
COKE	cocaine
COKE BUGS	experiencing the hallucination that bugs are crawling under the skin after using cocaine
COLD TURKEY	quitting a drug suddenly without the benefit of medication

COLOMBIAN .... a potent variety of marijuana grown in Colombia
CONTACT LENS ... LSD
CORAL .... chloral hydrate
COUNT .... the amount of purity of a drug
COP MAN .... a drug dealer (pusher)
CRACK .... purified cocaine sold in capsules
CRANK .... amphetamines
CRANK BUGS ..... the feeling that bugs are crawling under the skin after heavy amphetamine use
CRIS .... methamphetamine in powdered form
CRYSTAL .... cocaine crystals or methamphetamine in powdered form

DAGGA .... South African cannabis
DEW .... marijuana
DECK .... a folded paper containing heroin
DEXIES .... dexamphetamine tablets or capsules
DIME.............. ten dollars
DOLLAR........... one hundred dollars
DOWNER .... any depressant
DRAGGED .... a hysterical panic reaction after smoking marijuana
DRUGGIES .... people who experiment with a variety of drugs
DRY HIGH .... marijuana
DUST .... cocaine, angel dust
DUSTER .... tobacco and heroin mixed in a cigarette
DYNAMITE .... a particularly potent drug

EATER .... a person who takes drugs orally
ELECTRIC .... a punch containing LSD
   KOOL-ADE
ELEPHANT .... phencyclidine

FAKE A BLAST .... to pretend to be under the influence of a drug

FIFTEEN CENTS ...	fifteen dollars
FIT	paraphenalia for injection
FIX	the injecting of heroin, or the heroin itself
FLAKE	cocaine
FLAKY	a person who is addicted to cocaine
FLIP OUT	a panic reaction in which the user loses contact with reality
FLOATING	being under the effect of a drug
FLORIDA SNOW ...	fake cocaine
FLUNKY	one who takes foolish risks to obtain drugs
FLY	cocaine
FORWARDS	amphetamines
FOURS	Tylenol with codeine
FREAK OUT	a panic reaction to a drug
FREE BASE	a pure form of cocaine. Street cocaine is converted into free base by using chemical kits.
GANGA, GANJA ...	extremely potent marijuana grown in Jamaica
GANGSTER	marijuana
GANGSTER PILLS ..	barbiturates
GARBAGE	poor quality heroin
GARBAGE HEAD ..	a person who uses any available drug to get high
GERONIMO	a mixture of barbiturates and alcohol
GET OFF	to experience the effects of a drug
GIGGLE WEED	marijuana
GIRL	cocaine
GOOFBALL	amphetamine and barbiturate
GRASS	marijuana
GRIFA	marijuana
GRETA	marijuana
GUNJA	marijuana

H	heroin
HARRY	heroin
HASH	hashish
HAY	marijuana
HEAD	user of drugs, a high
HEAD DRUGS	drugs that affect the mind, such as LSD as opposed to narcotics
HEAVEN, HEAVEN DUST	cocaine
HIGH..............	euphoria
IDIOT PILLS.......	barbiturates
INDIAN HAY	marijuana
INDIAN HEMP	marijuana
IRON CURE	withdrawal without drugs
JAM	cocaine
JAMMED UP	a person who has taken an overdose
JANE	marijuana
JUANITA	Mexican term for marijuana
JOINT	marijuana cigarette
JOY POWDER......	heroin
JUNKIE	someone who uses heroin
KEY	a kilogram
KHAT	a stimulant milder than amphetamines that can produce psychological dependence
KILLER DRUGS....	drugs of high potency that are considered good
KILLER WEED	high potency marijuana or marijuana mixed with phencyclidine
KING KONG PILLS	barbiturates
KNOCK-OUT DROPS	a mixture of alcohol and chloral hydrate that produces loss of consciousness. There is an addictive affect.

LADY, LADY SNOW	cocaine
LEAPERS	amphetamines
LID	a measurement used for marijuana; enough marijuana to make about 40 cigarettes.
LOCO	marijuana
LUDES	quaaludes
MAGIC .... MUSHROOM	psilocybin
MAN, THE	can refer to the police or a high-level drug dealer
M AND C	a mixture of four parts morphine and one part cocaine
MARY	morphine
MARY ANN, ... MARY JANE, MARY WARNER, MARY WEAVER	marijuana
METH	methedrine, methamphetamine
MEXICAN BROWN .	marijuana grown in Mexico with high resin content, also brown heroin
MEXICAN GREEN .	one of the most common types of marijuana used in the United States, less potent than Mexican brown
MISS EMMA	morphine
MOOTA	marijuana
MU	marijuana
NARCOS	narcotics agents
NEMBIES	nembutal
NEEDLE FREAK ...	one who gets a thrill out of using a needle for drug injection without regard to the drug
NICKEL	five dollars
NOD	feeling the initial effects of a heroin injection

Nose Candy...... cocaine

O.................... opium
O.D. .... overdose
Oil .... hashish oil
Orange County . quaaludes, originating from the fact that
the code number on 300 mg. quaaludes
was the same as the area code for
Orange County
Overcharged ... a semi-conscious state resulting from too
much of a drug

Panama Gold, ... marijuana from Panama
    Panama Red
Panic .... an anxiety state resulting from shortage
of drugs
Paper acid .... LSD
Peace Pill .... phencyclidine
Peanuts .... barbiturates
Pearks............ amyl nitrate
Pellets .... LSD
Pep Pills......... amphetamines
Peyote Buttons . the buttonlike part of peyote cactus
Phennies .... phenobarbital
Pink Ladies ...... barbiturates
Pinks .... seconal
Pinned .... refers to constricted pupils of the eyes of
heroin addicts
Poppers .... amyl nitrate
Pot .... marijuana
Pot Head .... someone who uses marijuana often
Powder .... amphetamine in powdered form
Pusher .... a dealer who sells drugs to users

Quaaludes .... methaqualone
Quarter Bag .... twenty-five dollars worth of marijuana

QUILL .... a matchbook that is used to hold a drug while it is being sniffed

RAGWEED .... poor quality marijuana
RAINBOWS .... tuinal
RED BIRD, ... seconal sodium
  RED BULLETS,
  RED DEVILS,
  RED DOLLS,
  REDS
REEFER .... marijuana
ROACH .... a marijuana cigarette that has been burned down too far to be held by the fingers
ROCK .... cocaine or heroin
ROPE .... marijuana
ROYAL BLUE ...... LSD

SATIVA .... marijuana
SCAG .... heroin
SCHMACK .... drugs
SCHOOLBOY .... codiene, cocaine
SCRIPT .... prescription
SECCY .... seconal sodium
SHIT .... heroin
SHOOTING .... a place where people are injecting drugs
  GALLERY
SKAG .... heroin
SKIN .... the paper used for making marijuana cigarettes
SMACK .... heroin
SMOKE .... marijuana
SNORT .... the inhaling of powdered drugs
SNOW .... cocaine
SOPOR .... methaqualone
SPEED .... any stimulant

SPEED BALL ...... a mixture of a stimulant and sedative which is injected.

SPEED FREAK ..... a heavy user of amphetamines

SPLASH .... amphetamines

STAR DUST........ cocaine

STICK .... marijuana cigarette

STRUNG OUT ...... uncontrolled habitual use of a drug

SUPERGRASS .... phencyclidine, sometimes used for catnip sold as marijuana

SWEET LUCY...... marijuana

TABS .... LSD tablets or capsules

TALL .... high on a drug

TEA .... marijuana

TEXAS TEA .... marijuana

THC .... chemical derived from marijuana

TICKET............ drug used to provide a hallucinogenic "trip"

TIGHTEN UP ...... give drugs to a person

TOKE PIPES .... pipes used to smoke marijuana

TOOT .... to snort or sniff cocaine

TRAVEL AGENT ... a dealer who sells LSD

TRUCK DRIVERS .. amphetamines

TURP.............. terpin hydrate with codeine

UPPERS............ stimulants

USER .... a person who uses drugs

VIPE .... marijuana

WAKE UPS .... amphetamines

WALLBANGERS.... methaqualone

WEED............. marijuana

WHEAT .... marijuana

WHITE CROSSES .. amphetamines

WHITE .... LSD, moonshine
   LIGHTNING
WHITES .... benzedrine
WIPED OUT .... acute drug intoxication
WRECKED .... extremely high on drugs

YELLOW .... LSD
YELLOW BULLETS, nembutal
   YELLOW DOLLS,
   YELLOW
   JACKETS
YERBA .... marijuana

ZACATECAS .... potent marijuana grown in the Mexican
   PURPLE   state of Zacatecas
ZONKED .... acutely intoxicated by a drug

PSYCHOACTIVE DRUGS*

I. Drug, Trade or Other Names, Medical Uses

II. Drug, Physical Dependence, Psychological Dependence, Tolerance, Duration of Effect in Hours

III. Drug, Usual Methods of Administration, Possible Effects, Effects of Overdose, Withdrawal Syndrome

IV. Alcohol Effects

* Source: United States Drug Enforcement Administration

I. NARCOTICS

Opium	Dover's Powder, Paregoric, Parepectolin	Analgesic, antidiarrheal
Morphine	Morphine, Pectoral Syrup	Analgesic, antitussive
Codeine	Tylenol with Codeine, Empirin Compound with Codeine, Robitussan A-C	Analgesic, antitussive
Heroin	Diacetylmorphine, Horse, Smack	Under investigation
Hydromorphine	Dilaudid	Analgesic
Meperidine (Pethidine)	Demerol, Mepergan	Analgesic
Methodone	Dolophine, Methadone, Methadose	Analgesic
Other Narcotics	LAAM, Leritine, Numorphan, Percodan, Tussionex, Fentanyl, Darvon, Talwin, Lomotil	Analgesic, antidiarrheal, antitussive

I. DEPRESSANTS

Drug	Trade or Other Names	Medical Uses
Chloral Hydrate	Noctec, Somnos	Hypnotic
Barbiturates	Phenobarbital, Tuinal, Amytal, Nembutal, Seconal	Anesthetic, anticonvulsant, sedative, hypnotic
Benzodiazepines	Ativan, Azene, Clonopin, Dalmane, Diazepam, Librium, Xanax, Serax, Tranxene, Valium, Verstran, Halcion, Paxipam, Restoril	Anti-anxiety, anticonvulsant, sedative, hypnotic
Methaqualone	Parest, Quaalude	Sedative, hypnotic
Glutethimide	Doriden	Sedative, hypnotic
Other Depressants	Equanil, Miltown, Noludar, Placidyl, Valmid	Anti-anxiety, sedative, hypnotic

I. STIMULANTS

Drug	Trade or Other Names	Medical Uses
Cocaine*	Coke, Flake, Snow	Local anesthetic
Amphetamines	Biphetamine, Delcobese, Desoxyn, Dexedrine, Mediatric	Hyperkinesis, narcolepsy, weight control
Phenmetrazine	Preludin	Hyperkinesis, narcolepsy, weight control
Methylphenidate	Ritalin	Hyperkinesis, narcolepsy, weight control
Other Stimulants	Adipex, Bacarate, Cylert, Didrex, Ionamin, Plegine, Pre-Sate, Sanorex, Tenuate, Tepanil, Voranil	Hyperkinesis, narcolepsy, weight control

*Legally classified as a narcotic

I. HALLUCINOGENS

DRUG	TRADE OR OTHER NAMES	MEDICAL USES
LSD	Acid, Microdot	None
Mescaline and Peyote	Mesc, Buttons, Cactus	None
Amphetamine Variants	2.5-DMA, PMA, STP, MDA, MMDA, TMA, DOM, DOB	None
Phencyclidine	PCP, Angel Dust, Hog	Veterinary anesthetic
Phencyclidine Analogs	PCE, PCPy, TCP	None
Other Hallucinogens	Bufotenine, Ibogaine, DMT, DET, Psilocybin, Psilocyn	None

I. CANNABIS

DRUG	TRADE OR OTHER NAMES	MEDICAL USES
Marijuana	Pot, Acapulco Gold, Grass, Reefer, Sinsemilla, Thai Sticks	Under investigation
Tetrahydrocannabinol	THC	Under investigation
Hashish	Hash	None
Hashish Oil	Hash Oil	None

II. NARCOTICS

Drug	Physical Dependence	Psychological Dependence	Tolerence	Duration of Effect in Hrs.
Opium	High	High	Yes	3–6
Morphine	High	High	Yes	3–6
Codeine	Moderate	Moderate	Yes	3–6
Heroin	High	High	Yes	3–6
Hydromorphone	High	High	Yes	3–6
Meperidine (Pethidine)	High	High	Yes	3–6
Methadone	High	High-Low	Yes	12–24
Other Narcotics	High-Low	High-Low	Yes	Variable

II. DEPRESSANTS

Drug	Physical Dependence	Psychological Dependence	Tolerence	Duration of Effect in Hrs.
Chloral Hydrate	Moderate	Moderate	Yes	5-8
Barbiturates	High-Moderate	High-Moderate	Yes	1-16
Glutethimide	High	Moderate	Yes	4-8
Methaqualone	High	High	Yes	4-8
Benzodiazepines	Low	Low	Yes	4-8
Other Depressants	Moderate	Moderate	Yes	4-8

II. STIMULANTS

Drug	Physical Dependence	Psychological Dependence	Tolerence	Duration of Effect in Hrs.
Cocaine*	Possible	High	Yes	1–2
Amphetamines	Possible	High	Yes	2–4
Phenmetrazine	Possible	High	Yes	2–4
Methylphenidate	Possible	Moderate	Yes	2–4
Other Stimulants	Possible	High	Yes	2–4

*Legally classified as a narcotic

II. HALLUCINOGENS

Drug	Physical Dependence	Psychological Dependence	Tolerence	Duration of Effect in Hrs.
LSD	None	Degree unknown	Yes	8–12
Mescaline and Peyote	None	Degree unknown	Yes	8–12
Amphetamine Variants	Unknown	Degree unknown	Yes	Variable
Phencyclidine	Degree unknown	High	Yes	Days
Phencyclidine Analogs	Degree unknown	High	Yes	Days
Other Hallucinogens	None	Degree unknown	Possible	Variable

II. CANNABIS

DRUG	PHYSICAL DEPENDENCE	PSYCHOLOGICAL DEPENDENCE	TOLERENCE	DURATION OF EFFECT IN HRS.
Marijuana	Degree unknown	Moderate	Yes	2–4
Tetrahydrocannabinol	Degree unknown	Moderate	Yes	2–4
Hashish	Degree unknown	Moderate	Yes	2–4
Hashish Oil	Degree unknown	Moderate	Yes	2–4

III. NARCOTICS

DRUG	USUAL METHODS OF ADMINISTRATION	
Opium	Oral, smoked	*Possible Effects*—Euphoria, drowsiness, respiratory depression, constricted pupils, nausea
Morphine	Oral, injected, smoked	*Effects of Overdose*—Slow and shallow breathing, clammy skin, convulsions, coma, possible death
Codeine	Oral, injected	*Withdrawal Syndrome*—Watery eyes, runny nose, yawning, loss of appetite, irritability, tremors, panic, chills and sweating, cramps, nausea
Heroin	Injected, sniffed, smoked	
Hydromorphone	Oral, injected	
Meperidine (Pethidine)	Oral, injected	
Methadone	Oral, injected	
Other Narcotics	Oral, injected	

III. DEPRESSANTS

DRUG	USUAL METHODS OF ADMINISTRATION	
Chloral Hydrate	Oral	*Possible Effects*—Slurred speech, disorientation, drunken behavior without odor of alcohol
Barbiturates	Oral, injected	*Effects of Overdose*—Shallow respiration, clammy skin, dilated pupils, weak and rapid pulse, coma, possible death
Glutethimide	Oral, injected	*Withdrawal Syndrome*—Anxiety, insomnia, tremors, delirium, convulsions, possible death
Methaqualone	Oral, injected	
Benzodiazepines	Oral, injected	
Other Depressants	Oral, injected	

III. STIMULANTS

DRUG	USUAL METHODS OF ADMINISTRATION	
Cocaine	Sniffed, injected, smoked	*Possible Effects*—Increased alertness, excitation, euphoria, increased pulse rate and blood pressure, insomnia, loss of appetite
Amphetamines	Oral, injected	*Effects of Overdose*—Agitation, increase in body temperature, hallucinations, convulsions, possible death
Phenmetrazine	Oral, injected	*Withdrawal Syndrome*—Apathy, long periods of sleep, irritability, depression, disorientation
Methylphenidate	Oral, injected	
Other Stimulants	Oral, injected	

III. HALLUCINOGENS

DRUG	USUAL METHODS OF ADMINISTRATION	
LSD	Oral	*Possible Effects*—Illusions and hallucinations, poor perception of time and distance *Effects of Overdose*—Longer, more intense "trip" episodes, psychosis, possible death *Withdrawal Syndrome*—Withdrawal syndrome not reported
Mescaline and Peyote	Oral, injected	
Amphetamine Variants	Oral, injected	
Phencyclidine	Smoked, oral, injected	
Phencyclidine Analogs	Smoked, oral, injected	
Other Hallucinogens	Oral, injected, smoked, sniffed	

III. CANNABIS

Drug	Usual Methods of Administration	
Marijuana	Smoked, oral	*Possible Effects*—Euphoria, relaxed inhibitions, increased appetite, disoriented behavior
Tetrahydrocannabinol	Smoked, oral	*Effects of Overdose*—Fatigue, paranoia, possible psychosis
Hashish	Smoked, oral	*Withdrawal Syndrome*—Insomnia, hyperactivity, and decreased appetite occasionally reported
Hashish Oil	Smoked, oral	

IV. ALCOHOL EFFECTS

Trade Name	Chemical Name	Physical Dependence	Psychological Dependence	Tolerence	Duration of Effect in Hrs.	Usual Method of Administration
Beer, Ale, Malt Liquor	Ethyl Alcohol	High	Variable	Yes	Variable	Oral
Wine, Champagne, Wine Drinks	Ethyl Alcohol	High	Variable	Yes	Variable	Oral
Whiskey, Gin, "Hard Liquors"	Ethyl Alcohol	High	Variable	Yes	Variable	Oral

Usual Short-term Effects—Central nervous system depressant; relaxation (sedation); sometimes euphoria; impaired judgment, reaction time, coordination, and emotional control; frequent aggressive behavior and driving accidents

Usual Long-term Effects—Sometimes drowsiness, dryness of mouth, blurring of vision, skin rash, tremors; occasionally jaundice, agranulocytosis

SUGGESTIONS
FOR FURTHER
READING

Carroll, Marilyn. *PCP: The Dangerous Angel.* New York: Chelsea House, 1985.

Cohen, Miriam. *Marijuana: Its Effects on Mind and Body.* New York: Chelsea House, 1985.

Cohen, Sydney. *Cocaine: The Bottom Line.* Rockville, MD: The American Council for Drug Education, 1985.

Debner, Claudia Bialke. *Chemical Dependency: Opposing Viewpoints.* St. Paul, MN: Greenhaven Press, 1985.

Dolan, Edward F., Jr. *International Drug Traffic.* New York: Franklin Watts, 1985.

Gold, Mark S. *800-Cocaine.* New York: Bantam Books, 1984.

Golden, Sandy. *Driving the Drunk Off the Road.* Gaithersburg, MD: Quince Mill Books, 1983.

Grinspoon, Lester and Bakalar, James B. *Psychedelic Drugs Reconsidered.* New York: Basic Books, 1979.

Hawkins, John A. and Grab, Gerald N., (eds.). *Opium Addicts and Addiction.* Salem, NY: Ayer and Company, 1981.

Henningfield, Jack E. *Addiction.* New York: Chelsea House, 1985.

Hentoff, Nat. *A Doctor Among the Addicts.* Chicago: Rand McNally, 1968.

Hyde, Margaret O. *Alcohol: Drink or Drug?* New York: McGraw-Hill, 1974.

Jackson, Michael and Jackson, Bruce. *Doing Drugs.* New York: St. Martins Press/Marek, 1983.

Louria, D. B. *The Drug Scene.* New York: McGraw-Hill, 1968.

Lukas, Scott E. *Amphetamines: Danger in the Fast Lane.* New York: Chelsea House, 1985.

Moskowitz, Herbert, *Marijuana and Driving: A Review.* Rockville, MD: The American Council on Marijuana, 1981.

National Research Council Institute of Medicine. *Marijuana and Health.* Washington, D.C.: National Academic Press, 1982.

O'Brien, Robert and Chafetz, Morris, M.D. *The Encyclopedia of Alcoholism.* New York: Facts on File, 1982.

O'Brien, Robert and Cohen, Sidney. *The Encyclopedia of Drug Abuse.* New York: Facts on File, 1984.

Smith, David E. and Luce, John. *Love Needs Care.* Boston: Little, Brown & Co., 1971.

Snyder, Solomon H. *Uses of Marijuana.* New York: Oxford University Press, 1971.

Talor, L. B., Jr. *Driving High: The Hazards of Driving, Drinking and Drugs.* New York: Franklin Watts, 1983.

Trulson, Michael E. *LSD: Visions or Nightmares.* New York: Chelsea House, 1985.

Weiss, Ann E. *Over-the-Counter Drugs.* New York: Franklin Watts, 1984.

SOURCES
OF FURTHER
INFORMATION

The following provide free and low-cost material on mind drugs:

Al-Anon Family Group Headquarters
One Park Avenue
New York, New York, 10016

Alateen
One Park Avenue
New York, New York 10016

Alcoholics Anonymous
AA World Services
P.O. Box 459
Grand Central Station
New York, New York 10163

American Council for Drug Education
5820 Hubbard Drive
Rockville, Maryland 20852

Do-It-Now Foundation
P.O. Box 5115
Phoenix, Arizona 85010

Drug Enforcement Administration
Office of Public Affairs
1405 I Street, N.W.
Washington, D.C. 10537

M.A.D.D. (Mothers Against Drunk Driving)
P.O. Box 819100
Dallas, TX 75381

National Association on Drug Abuse Problems
355 Lexington Avenue
New York, New York 10017

National Clearinghouse for Alcohol Information
P.O. Box 2345
Rockville, Maryland 20857

National Clearinghouse for Drug Abuse Information
P.O. Box 416
Kensington, Maryland 20795

National Highway Traffic Safety Administration
400 Seventh Street, N.W.
Washington, D.C. 20590

RID (Remove Intoxicated Drivers)
P.O. Box 520
Schenectady, New York, 12301

SADD
Box 800
Marlboro, Massachusetts 01752

SADD's
CONTRACT FOR LIFE

The Students Against Driving Drunk
Contract Between Parent and Teenager

TEENAGER :

I agree to call you for advice and/or transportation at any hour, from any place, if I am ever in a situation where I have been drinking or a friend or date who is driving me has been drinking.

_____

Signature

PARENT:

I agree to come and get you at any hour, any place, no questions asked and no argument at any time, or I will pay for a taxi to bring you home safely. I expect we would discuss this issue at a later time.

I agree to seek safe, sober transportation home if I am ever in a situation where I have had too much to drink or a friend who is driving me has had too much to drink.

_____   _____

Date   Signature

INDEX

MARGARET O. HYDE, the editor of *Mind Drugs,* contributed several of the chapters and has updated others in this revised edition. Some of her earlier books include *Sexual Abuse: Let's Talk About It; AIDS: What Does It Mean to You?; Computers That Think?: The Search for Artificial Intelligence;* and for younger readers, *Know About Smoking* and *Know About Drugs.*

Separate chapters were written by Allan Y. Cohen, PH.D., Executive Director of Pacific Institute for Research and Evaluation; Duke D. Fisher, M.D. Neuropsychiatrist; William H. McGlothlin, Ph.D., Psychologist; J. Martin Myers, M.D., and Kenneth E. Appel, Ph.D., Psychiatrists. The chapter by David E. Smith, M.D., Toxicologist, Founder-Director of the Haight-Ashbury Free Medical Clinic and one of the world's leading authorities on psychoactive drugs, has been thoroughly revised.